RAISING TEENS
While They're Still In Preschool

Ronald T. Habermas

RAISING TEENS

While They're Still In Preschool

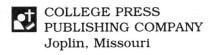

COLLEGE PRESS
PUBLISHING COMPANY
Joplin, Missouri

I lovingly dedicate this book to my parents, Robert and Roberta, who consistently fashioned an environment in our home — especially during my teen years — much like the Cities of Refuge in the Old Testament: a place that was always accessible, caring, hospitable, fair, and — above all — a place where I could fail safely.

Thanks, Dad and Mom, for giving Mary and me this great legacy, so that our three daughters now experience these same beneficiary blessings.

Brief Biographies
21 Experts for the 21st Century

Leith Anderson

Leith Anderson has been senior pastor of Wooddale Church in Eden Prairie, Minnesota since 1977. His education includes a Doctor of Ministry from Fuller Theological Seminary. His articles have been published in many periodicals and he has written several books including: *Mastering Church Management* (co-author; Multnomah), *Dying for Change* (Bethany), *A Church for the Twenty-First Century* (Bethany), *Who's in Charge?* (Co-author; Multnomah), *Winning the Values War* (Bethany) and *When God Says No* (Bethany). He has four adult children.

L. Dan Bautista

For the past year Dan has worked as a consultant in the areas of education and labor for LDB Consulting in Edinburg, Texas, while also founding and administering the Amigos Missionary Service. Four years prior to that time, Mr. Bautista served as an assistant to the President for Administration at Rio Grande Bible Institute in Edinburg.

While living in South Carolina, Dan provided leadership to that state's Department of Labor, maintaining the Executive

Director's position in the Farmworkers Division from 1992–1994. He also worked within the Associated Reformed Presbyterian Church, directing the Campus Ministry to Internationals at the University of South Carolina. In 1990, Mr. Bautista received his Master of Arts in Education at Columbia International University.

For ten years (1979–1988), Mr. Bautista was a board member of the Christian Camping Director's Association for the Latin-American Division, and in 1992 Dan was nominated to Who's Who among Hispanics in the U.S.

Mark Cannister

Mark is the Assistant Professor of Youth Ministries and the Chair of the Youth Ministries Program at Gordon College. He has a total of twenty-one years of youth ministry experience. He earned an Ed.D. degree in Social and Educational Theories at the University of Pittsburgh, and he serves on the board of the New England Network of Youth Workers. Mark is a husband and father of two kids.

Haman Cross, Jr.

Haman pastors the Rosedale Park Baptist Church, in Detroit, an urban congregation of well over 400 families. Haman and his wife, Roberta, are the parents of three adult children. He has published several books including *The Wild Thing, What's Up with Malcolm?, Have You Got Good Religion?, Fight Like a Man, Men to Men,* and *Cross Colors.* Haman has been a featured guest on several radio and television programs, such as *Focus on the Family, Talk from the Heart, Family Life Today* and *CTN Live!*

Roger Cross

Roger Cross serves as President of Youth for Christ in the United States. He has held that office since February, 1992. Earlier he served as the director of Youth for Christ Denver for 9 years and as the Executive Director of Ventura County Youth for Christ for 15 years. He and his wife, Jan, have two daughters and a foster son. Roger has been actively involved in discipling young people throughout his YFC ministry.

Ken Davis

Ken spent 15 years working in Youth for Christ and, in the last 20 years, has become one of the nation's top motivational and inspirational speakers. A wide variety of groups have teamed up with Ken Davis, including IBM, Focus on the Family, AT&T, Youth Specialties, Century 21, the Southern Baptist Convention, Burger King, the L.A. Police Dept., Service Master, and the American Bar Association. Ken has written seven books including, *How to Live with Your Parents without Losing Your Mind* and *How to Live with Your Kids When You've Already Lost Your Mind.* His books have received national critical acclaim including the Campus Life "Book of the Year" award and the CBA Gold Medallion Award. As president of Dynamic Communications, Ken provides seminars and a video series that teach speaking skills to ministry personnel and corporate executives. He and his wife, Diane, have two daughters, Taryn and Traci.

Richard R. Dunn

Rick Dunn is chair of the department of educational ministries and assistant professor of educational ministries at Trinity Evangelical Divinity School. He has been at Trinity since 1987 and has served in various youth ministry positions for almost 20 years. Rick was instrumental in developing Trinity's undergraduate youth ministry program.

Rick received both his Doctor of Education and the Master of Arts from Trinity Evangelical Divinity School. Since that time, he has co-edited *Reaching a Generation for Christ* (Moody, 1997). He has also written articles for parents and youth leaders, and has contributed to *The Life Application Bible for Students* (Tyndale, 1991) and *Keeping Your Kids Christian* (Servant, 1990). Mr. Dunn's areas of expertise include theology of youth ministry, the role of adults in the lives of youth, parenting teenagers, and basic leadership skills.

Rick and his wife, Teresa, live with their three children in Lake Villa, Illinois. In his spare time, he enjoys camping, traveling, and playing sports.

Len Kageler

Len is Professor of Youth Ministry and Christian Education at Nyack College, Nyack, New York. He was a youth pastor for 20 years prior to joining the faculty at Nyack. He and his wife, Janet, have three teenage daughters. Len has written several books, including three for parents: *How to Help Your Teenager Cope with Peer Pressure* (Group, 1989), *Teen Shaping* (Revell, 1990) and *On Being a Good Dad* (Revell, 1991). He has his Ph.D. in Sociology from Fordham University in New York City.

Jay Kesler

Jay Kesler is the president of Taylor University and host of the nationally-syndicated radio program, *Family Forum.* Jay is the author of nineteen books, including *Let's Succeed with Our Teenagers, I Want a Home with No Problems, Family Forum, Restoring a Loving Marriage, Grandparenting — The Agony and the Ecstasy, Challenges for the College Bound,* and *Being Holy, Being Human.* In addition, he has authored numerous magazine articles for publications such as *Christianity Today, Moody Monthly, Today's Christian Woman,* and *Sunday Digest.* Jay was president of Youth for Christ from 1973-85, and served that organization for a total of thirty years. Since Jay Kesler's 1985 arrival as president of his alma mater, Taylor has been listed ten times in the *U.S. News and World Report* survey *America's Best Colleges and Universities.* Jay and his wife, Jane, are the parents of three adult children and the grandparents of nine.

Marlene LeFever

Marlene LeFever is Manager of Ministry Relations for David C. Cook Church Ministries Group. She has authored over ten books, among them *Learning Styles — Reaching Everyone God Gave You to Teach* (Cook), *Creative Teaching Methods* (Cook), *Is Your*

To-Do List about to Do You In? (NavPress), and *Creative Hospitality* (Tyndale). Her Bible study books for children include *The Children's 50-Day Spiritual Journey 1985-1991* (Chapel Ministries). Past president of the Evangelical Press Association, Marlene's articles have appeared in many magazines and journals including *Evangelizing Today's Child, Decision, Moody Monthly, Christian Parenting Today, Single Adult Ministries Journal*, and *Youthworker Journal*. She was a member of the Princeton Seminary Summer faculty in 1981, visiting faculty member at Talbot Theological Seminary (1983), Denver Seminary (1987), and Canadian Bible College (1993). Each year Marlene speaks to over 10,000 church Christian education volunteers. She has done cross-cultural Christian education in Mexico City and Manila, and has led Christian education seminars in Austria, England, Northern Ireland, and Scotland.

Dennis "Tiger" McCluen

Since 1988 Dennis has been the Executive Director of Youth Leadership Center for Youth and Family Ministry in Minneapolis. He is married, with three children. His education includes an MACE degree from Bethel Theological Seminary. Dennis oversees the youth ministry program at Bethel and Luther Seminaries, where he teaches all the youth ministry courses at both schools. He has over 22 years of youth ministry experience. Dennis is the author of *Equipped to Serve*, a youth ministry volunteer training course.

Helen Musick

Helen Musick teaches Youth Ministry at Asbury Seminary in Wilmore, Kentucky. She is a member of the Youth Specialties National Resource Team. Helen's ministry experience ranges from working with female juvenile offenders in a local prison ministry to leading local youth ministry.

Helen has published several youth ministry resources. She frequently speaks across the country to youth and adults.

She and her husband, John, have three children: Nathan, Laura, and Will.

David Olshine

David is the Chairman of the Youth Ministry Department at Columbia International University in Columbia, South Carolina. David received his Doctor of Ministry degree in Family Systems from Eastern Baptist Seminary. David was raised Jewish and gave his life to Jesus the Messiah at the age of eighteen. For the past nineteen years David has been actively involved in youth ministry. David is the author of *Staying on Top*, a workbook on Philippians. His newest books are *Down-But-Not-Out Parenting, Tag-Team Youth Ministry*, (co-authored with Ron Habermas) and *Actual Reality* (co-authored with Helen Musick), published by Standard. David speaks to over 15,000 youth, youth workers and parents of teens annually. David is married to Rhonda and has one teenage daughter, Rachel.

Ginny Olson

Ginny Olson is the director of the Youth Ministry Department at North Park University in Chicago, Illinois. She is also the director of Young Adult Ministries for the Evangelical Covenant Church. Currently, she volunteers her time as the president of the Association of Women in Youth Ministry. Along with the former president, Diane Elliot, they are the co-editors of the book, *Breaking the Gender Barrier in Youth Ministry*. Previous to her work at North Park, Ginny was an associate director in Willow Creek Community Church's junior high ministry. She has a M.A. in Educational Ministries from Wheaton Graduate School, in Illinois, where her thesis researched why youth pastors leave youth ministry.

Les Parrott

Les Parrott is a professor of psychology and co-director (with his wife Leslie) of the Center for Relationship Development at Seattle Pacific University. Les earned his M.A. in theology and Ph.D. in clinical psychology from Fuller Theological Seminary. Each year, he speaks to thousands of people in a variety of settings across North America and around the world. He has written several best-selling books including *Helping the Struggling Adolescent, Seven Secrets of a Healthy Dating Relationship, High-Maintenance Relationships,* and the award-winning *Saving Your Marriage Before It Starts.* His McGraw-Hill textbook, *Counseling and Psychotherapy,* is used in numerous college and university courses. In addition to countless radio appearances, Les's work has been featured in such newspapers as *USA Today* and the *Chicago Tribune.* His television appearances include CNN and Oprah. His articles have appeared in such magazines as *Christianity Today, Marriage Partnership, Moody, Aspire, Virtue, Group, New Man,* and *Focus on the Family.*

Dave Rahn

Dave Rahn is Professor of Educational Ministries, Associate Dean for Graduate Studies, and co-director of the Link Institute... for faithful and effective youth ministry at Huntington College. Prior to coming to Huntington in 1985, he served as Campus Life club director, ministry coordinator, and training director with the Fort Wayne Area Youth for Christ for 13 years. Dave has served as a consultant to church and parachurch organizations, and he speaks frequently in a variety of settings. Dave received a Ph.D. from Purdue University in Educational Studies—Social/Moral Development. He has published numerous articles, including some related to cooperative learning, professionalism in youth ministry, the effectiveness of big events in youth ministry, and youth ministry training. He and his wife, Susie, have two young teens, Jason and Alison. Dave still volunteers in a local Campus Life outreach, involving about 150 high schoolers weekly.

Wayne Rice

Wayne Rice is currently the president of Understanding Your Teenager, an organization serving parents of teens and preteens. He is also the cofounder of Youth Specialties, a nondenominational organization which provides resources and training for youth workers. Wayne has worked with youth since 1963 in church and parachurch youth ministry. He has authored numerous books about youth and youth ministry, including *Junior High Ministry* (1978, rev. 1987), *Great Ideas for Small Youth Groups* (1985), *Up Close and Personal* (1989), *Hot Illustrations for Youth Talks* (1994), *Enjoy Your Middle Schooler* (1994), and *More Hot Illustrations for Youth Talks* (1996). Wayne has also served as editor of *Youthworker Journal*, *Youthworker Update* newsletter, and *Ideas* magazine, published by Youth Specialties. He and Miles McPherson co-authored *One Kid at a Time* (1995), a book/video curriculum on mentoring teenagers. Wayne also directs the youth mentoring program at Shadow Mountain Community Church, El Cajon, California. A graduate of Bethel Theological Seminary (MATS), Wayne is currently a Faculty Associate in Youth Ministry at Bethel Theological Seminary, West Campus and is a frequent guest lecturer at colleges and seminaries in the U.S. and Canada. Wayne's "avocation" is bluegrass music. He was an original member of the group "Brush Arbor" which was voted Vocal Group of the Year at the Academy of Country Music Awards (1973). Since 1976, he has hosted a weekly radio program called "The Bluegrass Special" on KSON AM/FM, San Diego's country-music station. Wayne and his wife, Marci, have three children: Nathan, Amber and Corey who have each passed their teen years.

Mark H. Senter, III

Mark H. Senter, III is Vice President and Dean of the Division of Open Studies and Associate Professor of Christian Education at Trinity Evangelical Divinity School in Deerfield, Illinois. He has been at Trinity since 1982. Prior to that, Mark served as youth pastor for 11 years and as pastor of Christian education at Wheaton Bible Church for seven years. Mark earned his Ph.D. in Foundations of Education from Loyola University in Chicago. His publications include: *Reaching a Generation for Christ* (co-edited with Richard Dunn) (Moody 1997); *The Coming Revolution in Youth Ministry* (Victor 1992); *Recruiting Volunteers in the Church* (Victor 1990); and *The Complete Book of Youth Ministry* (co-edited with Warren

Benson) (Moody 1987), and numerous articles have been published in many well-known periodicals. Mark and his wife, Ruth, reside in north suburban Chicago. They have two grown children.

Thom Schultz

Thom is the president of Group Publishing, Inc., based in Loveland, Colorado. Group services more than 200,000 church workers and millions of children and young people, worldwide. He founded Group Publishing, in 1974, which produces three leading magazines: *Group, Jr. High Ministry,* and *Children's Ministry.* Thom's ministry organizes and sponsors a variety of events: the National Youth and Children's Ministry Convention, Group Workcamps, and Children's Ministry Workshop. Thom is the co-author of *Why Nobody Learns Much of Anything at Church: And How to Fix It, Involving Youth in Youth Ministry,* and *Do It! Active Learning in Youth Ministry.* He has written scores of articles on Christian education and youth ministry, and his column ("Youth Ministry Minute") appears in each issue of *Group Magazine.* He's been active in youth ministry and Christian education for over 20 years.

Harold Ivan Smith

Harold is president of Harold Ivan Smith and Associates, a consulting firm that offers leadership in the areas of single adult issues, grief, and spiritual formation. Harold has a Ed.S. degree from Vanderbilt University, and he received the Doctor of Ministry in spiritual formation from Asbury Theological Seminary. He also holds the Doctor of Ministry in pastoral care from Luther Rice Seminary. Harold's recent publication is called *Deepening the Path: Spirituality for Single Adults* (Abingdon). Other, recent writings include: *Fifty-One Good Things to Do While Waiting for the Right One to Come Along,* and *Reluctantly Single.* He has also authored the innovative nine-week divorce recovery program, *A Time for Healing: Coming to Terms with Your Divorce* published by Lifeway. Harold is an adjunct professor of single adult ministry at Northern Baptist Theological Seminary and has served on the Board of the

Network of Single Adult Leaders. Smith's speaking and research has taken him to Haiti, England, Italy, China, Hong Kong, Turkey, Israel, and Bosnia.

Mike Yaconelli

Mike Yaconelli has been working with young people for 36 years. He is owner of Youth Specialties, an international organization that trains and provides resources for over 100,000 youth workers worldwide. Youth Specialties was co-founded by Mike Yaconelli and Wayne Rice back in 1968. Mike lives in Yreka, California, a rural northern California town where he is lay pastor of Grace Community Church, a small church "for those who don't like church." He and his wife, Karla, are now discovering what it is like to adjust to a cavernous house where their five adult children Mark, Trent, Lisa, Jill, and Jessica used to live. Mike is a local high school board member and the proud grandfather of Noah. He breezed through his four-year college education in ten years and finally graduated from San Diego State University with a degree in communications.

Table of Contents

Introduction   19

Chapter 1 • Backdrop of Contemporary
                Culture and Families   23

Chapter 2 • Roadblocks & Bridges   47

Chapter 3 • Advice for All Caregivers   65

Chapter 4 • "Musts" of Christian Parenting   87

Chapter 5 • Marooned Like Gilligan
                (Helpful Resources)   101

Chapter 6 • Insights for Single Parents   109

Chapter 7 • What Your Teen Needs to Hear   127

Chapter 8 • Favorite Tidbits of Wisdom   141

Chapter 9 • Encouraging Your Child's Spiritual Walk   153

Chapter 10 • Stepping Back into Time   173

Chapter 11 • Hope for Blended Families   185

Chapter 12 • The "D" Word — Discipline   195

Chapter 13 • Recharging Your Batteries   209

Chapter 14 • Waving a Magic Wand   223

Chapter 15 • What Lies Ahead?   237

Conclusion   255

Bibliography • References Cited   263

Introduction

Two urgent and powerful demands from our culture drive me to create this practical resource for parents. The first pressing demand is *relevance*, which cannot possibly be overstated, as illustrated by the following questions:

What do these recent dates hold in common: October 1, 1997; December 1, 1997; March 24, 1998; April 24, 1998; May 1, 1998; and May 19, 1998?

Give up?

Would it help if I provided these six respective geographical sites, as clues: Pearl, Mississippi; Paducah, Kentucky; Jonesboro, Arkansas; Edinboro, Pennsylvania; Springfield, Oregon; and Fayetteville, Tennessee?

Yes, each of these half-dozen dates and cities represent tragic settings of the nationwide public school shootings in 1997–1998.

I certainly don't review these for either mere trivia recall or sensationalism. In fact, I can't personally revisit these senseless killings without a conscious soberness of mind and dull pain in my heart. But I do raise these all-too-familiar current events as an indication of our all-too-sick society, in desperate need of healing.

Oh, yes, I also play back the tape on these six tragedies

because — on May 22, 1998, in our own Siloam Springs, Arkansas Middle School — a young boy threatened to bring a gun to school on the last day of classes to end the life of the principal.

Fortunately, it never happened. Yet, as my wife and I purposefully kept our youngest daughter home from school that Friday morning, I couldn't help but feel — throughout that entire day — the same despair I sensed when I was exactly my youngest's age. I'll never forget that earlier afternoon, thirty-five years ago, when I was walking the halls of my own junior high and heard over the PA system that John F. Kennedy had been assassinated.

By way of contrast with 1963, millions of people today have confronted *frequent and repeated encounters of anxiety and despair, all throughout the many months this past school year.* Besides the children and their teachers, no other section of our population has been jolted as hard as we who are parents.

The second reason which led me to create this resource is *ignorance.* Parents whose kids are slightly older than yours often tend to play the universally-known "Just Wait" game. When you show these folks your darling infant, they give you that "Havelgotnewsforyou" look and reply "Justwaitforthoseterribletwos."

Of course, such predictable naysayers don't stop there. They continue to play the "Just Wait" game — *ad nauseam* — until that final trump card known as "Waittiltheybecometeens!" Of course, with the circular reasoning on their side, you — the recipient — appear to lose two ways: first, you're implicitly told that you'll never "make it," since you're destined for one purpose, and one purpose only: to fatalistically and passively wait for each subsequent stage of parenting to unravel. Second, it's assumed that you're incapable of ever preparing for that next stage.

Both inferences are lies. Both are indicators of ignorance.

The curse of continuously holding our breath for tomorrow's challenges — especially motivated by anxiety or fear — is bogus. Furthermore, *we can adequately prepare, train and strengthen ourselves, as caregivers, for impending domestic stages.* As a parent of three children who've reached 21, 17, and 13 years of age, I stake my experience (and modest success) on those two facts.

But now, based on the research I was privileged to complete last year, *I also have twenty-one experts to back me up.* I interviewed key church and parachurch leaders who provided practical insights on how to parent teens. Although their comments were diverse — sometimes even contradictory — they all agreed on this single truth: **Successful parenting of teens requires successful parenting of young children. Serving preschoolers well today sets us on the right course for ministering to adolescents tomorrow.**

Now for a few necessary disclaimers:

✗ This book does *not* offer quick-fix solutions to the complex societal problems, like violence, noted above;

✗ This book does *not* promise a safe and pleasant journey as you navigate the turbulence of parenting teens; and

✗ This book does *not* even guarantee that your kids will turn out the way you hope they will.

No book — not Scripture itself — makes those claims! Don't let anybody convince you otherwise.

But I do promise the following useful benefits to any open-minded parent or concerned individual:

✓ Experts who will speak to you with **precision and honesty** — about both the blessings and the heartaches of parenting;

✓ Experienced parents and professionals who will offer **concise, keen insights** for you who are moms and dads — with virtually every piece of their advice fashioned as ready-to-use in everyday life; and

✓ Evangelical leaders who will probably **surprise** many of you readers with their fresh humor, wisdom, and down-to-earth reality checks which promote healthy Christian families.

For example, take a quick peek at several portions of the provocative ideas that were shared by these twenty-one experts:

☞ **"Parenting is overrated."**

☞ "Following Jesus is going to radically alter a kid's future. And, to be honest, most parents really don't want that."

☞ "Laugh a lot. Don't be afraid to celebrate."

☞ **"Date your kids."**

☞ "We've got a generation of fatigued parents who, when they get home, are spiritually empty. Spiritual cowards, perhaps."

☞ **"It's okay to be excited about Jesus."**

☞ "Parents often forget the power of the eavesdropper."

☞ "My dad honored me by laughing at my jokes."

☞ **"Sports today is nothing but treating people like they're a piece of meat. Why support this?"**

☞ **"Our culture is growing introverted — Bat Cave mentality."**

☞ "The fearful parent is an ineffective parent."

In sum, these representative citations reveal what this publication is all about: *A spiritually sensitive, cut-through-the jargon, street-wise guidebook. Furthermore, it provides an unusual blend of 2-resources-in-1. It offers explicit help to parents who currently have adolescents under their roof, and proactive assistance to caretakers who will, one day, have teens.*

So, if you're intrigued by the quotes you've just read, read on. Now you've got 21 godly men and women who are standing in your corner. Twenty-one good reasons, as a parent, to confidently head into the 21st century.

Dr. Ron Habermas
Siloam Springs, AR
June 1, 1998

Chapter 1
Backdrop of Contemporary Culture and Families

Paint some broad brushstrokes which express the adolescent culture and their homes. What are the current trends, you see today, both positive and negative?

Leith Anderson

We've gone through this period of Baby Boomers having children late, and having fewer children, and being significantly focused on those children. What we're going to see is the impact of that, for good and ill, coming into the teenage years. **Kids are growing up with fewer siblings.** They are very much the center of attention from their parents. The teenagers of the first part of the next century, if the economic trends continue, will be in a period of economic prosperity and peace and that, typically, is a period of significant freedom. People will not be drafted; that's going to differentiate them from other nations that have had wars and recessions. **We are going to see more and more teens who are the products of large churches because of a significant shift of population away from smaller churches into larger churches. And teens who come out of larger churches are very different than those who come out of smaller churches.**

Wayne Rice

The word "abandonment" rises to the top of the list of key words. I think kids have been abandoned by their parents, abandoned by our culture, and by society in general. **Most adults hate teenagers.** That has had a tremendous downward, spiraling effect. A vicious circle. Kids behave a certain way, and so adults reject them. That causes them to continue to behave a certain way, which causes adults to reject them even more. It keeps perpetuating itself. There's a cycle that somebody has to break somewhere along the line. That break should come where the adult world says, "We care about teenagers enough to stop manipulating them, stop exploiting them, stop abandoning them."

A cultural shift has occurred, where adolescents are separated more and more from the adult world. Prior to World War II, teenagers were viewed more as part of the adult world; they were young adults. But now, they're not ever young adults. They are teenagers, and teenage years are seen as a separate stage of life. It never was in the past. So, because they are no longer a part of the adult world, there are all kinds of problems with the teen culture. For instance, their ability to become responsible, self-reliant adults. It's really unfortunate. **It's a wholesale abandonment of teenagers by adults. Parents fear their kids. They're afraid of having teenagers in their own home.** They're really afraid of other teens, so they become afraid of their own kids. **Kids no longer have a place in the adult world to work, to contribute, and to use their gifts and talents. They're not needed as they were in the past.** Those are big negatives.

Thom Schultz

This crop of young people has looked on family issues and has seen the destruction and heartache caused by failed marriages. **These teens really understand the seriousness of marriage. They understand that it's not to be taken lightly. It's a big decision, and if the decision is made poorly, a lot of pain can be caused down the road. Consequently, they are waiting longer to get**

married. At the same time, young people today are more promiscuous. They are entering into serious relationships, but because of their promiscuity, these social ties are risky, supercharged with all of the emotions that are present on a sexual level. **Youth are going through what some people might call 'mini-divorces' — relationships that are powerful but often involve some degree of heartache.** Yes, they are avoiding marrying early, but they are also experiencing various kinds of heartache through broken relationships.

Another trend is the hyper-busyness in families, today. That causes some bitterness, both from the kids' point of view and the parents' point of view, some real grinding of emotions. You see it in the *Home Alone* movies — an illustration of a society that is too busy.

David Olshine

One trend that looks extremely positive (but could be extremely negative) is the onslaught of technomania — the increasing technological advances like computers and e-mail. **Our culture is crazed over gadgets. It looks positive, since this trend seems to be an avenue for greater communication. But what I see is greater introversion, turning *away* from people rather than turning *toward* people. We're going to see a lot of this in the future: kids going nuts over the Internet, but communicating less and less with their parents.** Another broad brushstroke that is shaping culture and affecting homes is increasing busyness. Busyness looks like godliness, but it's not. For example, my daughter, who's 13 years old, has never known life without microwaves and VCRs. And busyness.

Our culture is crazed over gadgets.

On a positive note, I think the church is finally addressing parents of teenagers.

Helen Musick

As far as the youth culture goes, and how that affects your home, **I think the negative is an absence of absolutes.** That's a pretty big change in our culture. I don't see it as a teenager's fault; I see it as something that has been passed down to them. **Absence of absolutes is just so huge. When you have no plumb line to judge what is right and what is wrong, then you have a complete breakdown of society.** So really everything, for me, stems from that. Of course, for positive trends, even in politics, we've got to recognize family values. With regard to what's happening in family, we see related issues: what's actually happening in education, the rise in teenage pregnancy and murder, suicide, gangs, and so forth.

Ken Davis

Many of the families today have both parents working, and they lack influence in the home. Also that television has had a major impact on the home. Those two are very related. **What time was ever historically spent in communication, even if it was not all positive communication — you know the "Leave It to Beaver" kind of communication — is almost all gone now. Television has had a tremendous impact on kids. Their peers, their music, and the media are what form teen lives.**

Marlene LeFever

The positive trend is that these contemporary youth (some call them "Millennial") are a lot more educationally savvy, than the group that we call " Gen X." They are hard working; they are more parent-dependent than the two generations before them. And I see those facts as extremely positive. **Millennials seem to realize what Gen Xers have realized lately: that the world has changed, and they are going to have to make some concessions.**

Ron Habermas: What's an example?

ML: Gen Xers grew up with more wealth and more privilege than any other generation. Yet when they became adults, all of a sudden they realized they couldn't attain what they had hoped they would be. It became a real negative for them. Their whole idea of reality stems from the fact that their original, anticipated goals would never be realized.

But this younger generation is not going through that. They grew up knowing that life was not going to be "business as usual." They are more open to paradigm shift; in fact, they think in paradigm shift. Another thing that is positive: their minds tend to think in short blasts of information, rather than in more linear patterns. Those of us who are older tend to think, "1,2,3,4, and therefore 5 comes next." You don't find that with them; you find more of a computer mind, an altogether different change in how people process information.

I'm not sure what that means, but it is opening a whole new way of looking at the Millennial. They're very protected youngsters. **Millennials will probably benefit from all the school reforms they've experienced. Smarter, better behaved, more civic-spirited than their immediate elders.** They will probably get very involved in communities — as the civic-doers and builders — taking over the same characteristic traits that people who went through World War II had.

Also, Millennials are technical geniuses. They can take the vision that people have and make it a reality. So the Boomers will look to this current generation (as well as Generation X) to do with technology what they could only dream. **They're dream-fulfillers.** I see that as a very positive thing.

Negatively, the older generation has no idea how to work with the new ways in which these youths think. We're not as picture literate. We think literally rather than asymmetrically. We're tied to traditional thought patterns, and I think that may hold this present generation back. We may have to wait until they're teachers to know how to deal with their children, because we sure don't know how to do it.

Millennials are technical geniuses.

Les Parrott

The biggest brushstroke that I see is a sense of apathy. It's depicted in their music, if you listen to something like *Smashing Pumpkins* or **Billy Corogan**, who tends to be a spokesperson for that generation. A true expression of complete apathy.

Ginny Olson

The most prominent elements in today's family culture are lack of intimacy and communication within the family. The rise of technology and computers and even computer games. Kids are communicating with a wire or with an impersonal person. They have not learned the face-to-face skills. And with parents becoming more and more busy, there's very little "let's get together with each other and talk." At best, it's parent and teen sitting in front of the TV, side-by-side. That's going to take its toll. Lack of communication with kids.

RH: I'm wondering if, when we do have human relationships in the future, they will have shortcomings because of these "TV tube" relationships. For example, will there be more superficiality? Are there other features that we haven't even thought about?

GO: Doug Rushcoff has a book called *Playing the Future*; it's a great one. He's the one who wrote *Gen X Reader* and *Media Virus*. The subtitle is, *How Kids' Culture Can Teach Us to Drive in the Age of Chaos*. He talks about how kids are so astute with technology. Where technology is very chaotic to adults, kids are making sense of it. How they pick and choose. **If they don't like a channel they use the remote. If they don't like the computer game they are playing, they switch levels, or they switch games. The implication is that, for relationships I don't like, I switch. I walk off.**

RH: A whole new dimension to the breakdown of the family. Anything else that you see as a trend?

GO: A trend of fear. The ramifications of kids growing up fearful of school. They're afraid to go to school. I may be more attuned to this because I work with city kids right now. But even when I worked at Willow Creek, I worked in a small group of sixth grade girls, and most of them knew of somebody who had brought a gun to school. They live with a low level of fear every day. They live with a low level of fear of even going home. "If I walk home, am I going to get beat up, am I going to encounter gangs?" Especially with younger kids. Then at home, it's not always roses either, if there is conflict there. Where is a safe place?

RH: Are there any positive trends?

GO: Parents are seeing that they need to increase their parenting skills. **Especially with Generation X, there is a hunger for community. They were latchkey kids, so they are saying: "I will not sacrifice my life for the corporation, like my parents did. Family is important to me, and consequently, I'm not putting in these long hours."** I think those are positive.

Roger Cross

One new trend which can be very positive is a coming generation that is rejecting some of the old answers. A subtle rejection of materialism — that it's the answer to all ills. Kids are also seeing the holes in what so many from my generation are involved in — success, getting the job, and so forth. I think kids are asking tough questions. I'm not sure that they're asking the right people the right questions but, at least, I see some answers they're not accepting.

RH: That's a good distinction. It's one thing to ask the right questions, and it's another thing to get the source for the right answers.

RC: Also, I see kids in many other countries growing up in a totally different environment than teens in the United States. We see a growing number of kids around the world that are strongly influenced by the political surroundings. And we don't have that extreme problem here in the United States. For instance, I read a report recently that, in Bosnia, 95% of the young people consider suicide. That's caused by a dynamic that we don't have here. So when we talk about young people, we can't judge all kids by what we see in the West.

RH: Let me play on that former statement that you made concerning the rethinking of old answers. Do you find that youth are not just questioning culture, but questioning the church?

RC: Oh sure. Absolutely. **One of the statistics that the Barna Group has reported is that 72% of kids from the church don't necessarily believe in absolute truth. That's certainly different. Teens are questioning absolutes.**

The Barna Group has reported that 72% of kids from the church don't necessarily believe in absolute truth.

RH: Any *good* examples of questioning in the church? Healthy questioning?

RC: Kids are basically asking questions about why things are done the way they're done. And people who have been in leadership don't necessarily know the answers to those inquiries. They just say, "Because that's the way we do it." Now, that's a threatening question. But, in the long run, if the church will allow themselves to grapple with those questions and say, 'Why are we doing this? Do we need to change? Is there a legitimate reason why we are preaching this particular virtue?" I think the end result will be good. But, in the meantime, it's a threatening situation.

Dave Rahn

Our society is being split down the middle by the culture wars, especially the view of authority. One side views moral authority that only comes from within. That's not just a teenage issue, it's an adult issue. There are parents who struggle with laying down the law or asking their teenager to obey them, because they are not certain they believe in a source of moral authority that's outside of the youth themselves. External authority. It's an erosion of the family authority structures.

RH: Besides authority, are there other culture war themes?

DR: Sensitivity to values. **Teens are more exposed to the progressive side of the culture wars, where values are considered with respect to the individuals. Individual self-fulfillment becomes a primary motivation.** The conservative side of the culture wars still says there's a right and a wrong. It's connected to the authority issue, but it's different. In a recent editorial page, columnist Cal Thomas talked about the new role for truth. Truth is no longer seen as something that you fall back on. You state the truth, and if it doesn't work, then you say, "Well, I gave it a shot." There's no backup. It's sort of like, if you claim it's true, it must be true unless you've proven otherwise. There's no root system to truth that can be verified. The world of teenage values is like that system.

RH: How about the positive side of our culture?

DR: We are moving toward a time that may parallel the 1960's trend of activism with teens. Teens are becoming more open to important causes — to something that makes a real difference. And less drawn to the model of the recent times: do your own thing and have your own fun.

Mike Yaconelli

In terms of youth ministry in the church, we've created our own monster. We have professionalized youth ministry, legitimized it to the point that now youth ministry is something that is done by somebody else and done separately from the life of the church. The result is that we hire a youth director or get some volunteers to do youth ministry. The church uses its support, then, financially and psychologically. But they don't really support it with their actual life, with who they are. **Parents see youth work as an enhancement to a kid's life. In other words, one of the big problems that I hear over and over again from youth workers is that the greatest obstacle for getting kids to come to youth group is the parents!** I just heard a parent say today, "I'm trying to get my daughter to go to church, but she has drill team; she has dance class; she has flute practice; she has soccer. And you know, it's tough to get all of those things in, and then get youth group in."

Really, what parents are wanting is for a youth group to be there when they can squeeze it into their schedule. It enhances kids' lives, so that they don't drink and don't smoke and don't get pregnant, and sort of go to church and believe in God and become nice, positive, suburban Americans. **Unfortunately, that's not what youth ministry should be about. The reality is that, when we introduce kids to Jesus, it is going to turn their life upside-down. They're not going to fit into this culture. They're probably going to question a whole lot of things**, like "Why am I going to college?"

Following Jesus is going to radically alter this kid's future. And, to be honest, parents really don't want that.

and "Why am I getting a degree and what is the point of all this?" And it's going to create tension in the family rather than make it all wonderful. **Following Jesus is going to radically alter this kid's future. And, to be honest, parents really don't want that.** They want a youth group that makes things more comfortable. Better, not worse.

And to that extent, they are very happy to support youth ministry as an enhancement to what they are doing; nothing too serious.

RH: So, your critique is positioning "enhancement" against what you're calling the "radical" approach — that should come from legitimate youth ministry?

MY: Yes, the whole emphasis today is on family values and on the fact that we support the family (and certainly we think the family is important). But it's not the most important thing. **In fact, biblically, it's very clear that when people follow Jesus, family is one of the casualties. Commitment actually creates rifts in families and doesn't always bring people together.** But that's not a big concern, because we believe in the power of the church. If my dad and my mom aren't functioning as they should, then I have the church that I can fall back on. That is where my real family is. Yet that is a minority viewpoint today. What parents really do not want is a youth ministry to be a place where their kids are disturbed or made uncomfortable with the way life is. But that's actually the proper definition of Christianity, so there's really not much we can do about that.

RH: So, you're not really defining the church in conventional terms. You're defining the church as people who question, people who also have a counterculture view of life — a value system that would shake people up. It's not just a focus on the teen and on the parent. You have a bigger view of this thing called the church?

MY: Of course. Sure I do. My view is that **kids are not the church of tomorrow, they're the church right now. We always say that.**

It's a very trite and so, therefore, a meaningless statement. **But, in reality, it's very true. Kids are the church now. They have great gifts for the church now.** And they need the adult modeling of the church now. They need friendships and relationships with people who believe in them, who care about them. That is critically important to these kids surviving in the future.

RH: Given those definitions of youth ministry and of the church, in particular, what signs of hope, what positive trends, do you recognize?

MY: When we talk about reality, we have to realize that there is a kind of consciousness. **Scott Peck says that sin is inertia. I love that because I think he really defines sin in a way that makes most of us uncomfortable.** When culture has its own momentum, when culture is moving in the direction our culture is moving, to try to stop, to try to get off the boat, to try to turn around and go the other way is so hard! It is so difficult. It takes great courage and resistance.

RH: First, there needs to be an awareness.

MY: Yes, first consciousness. But my take on it is that people are very conscious that something is wrong in our culture. They're very conscious that, yeah, in fact, this is not what ought to be. **Our souls are reacting to what our minds know. So, when I know that I'm isolated, my life has no meaning.** I'm too busy. I'm full of hectic activity, but doing nothing that really matters. My mind knows that. Then my soul longs for community, quiet, solitude, and relationship. **So now we have a society of people who are longing for family, for connectedness. To get off the treadmill, to quiet down.** For spirituality, of course — not just Christianity, but a broader sense of connecting with God.

I think people know this. I think more and more people are knowing this in their heart, not just in their mind. **But I really don't see much of a momentum building for people to finally say that we have to change. Beneath all that there is a kind of tiredness and, as a result, fatigue. People saying "I can't do this anymore. I've got to live life in a different way."**

Haman Cross

The explosion of technology will be the greatest single influence in the decades ahead. Everything is moving towards virtual reality. **Kids grow up with the sense of "instant" everything. We thought microwaves were fast. Whatever you want, you can have it, before you want it. It's sort of like a TV channel surfing scenario, except it ends up preventing a kid from being a kid before their teenage years.** Like the ten-year-old who should not have been exposed to a cult or a sensitive moral matter. **Instant access ruins our kids.** Get your money now. If you don't have it, then take it. Sex now. Power now. They will get used to having what they want — now! **They need to enjoy being young. Then, when they get old, they never need to say they didn't have the chance to be a kid.**

Rick Dunn

In terms of the positive, we have gone through a cultural stage where relationships have been valued, and I think that is a helpful trend. I'm not sure how it will translate into our parenting, but the fact that people recognize relationships — in a technologically advanced culture — shows that there is a hunger for people connections. And, potentially, the home is a place where teens can find this to be a very attractive commodity.

Second, **our culture has begun to recognize and validate adolescence experiences —** primarily because there is so much pain, like teen pregnancy or alcohol abuse or violence. If you watch the programming of the media, you see things like adolescents' perceptions, feelings, and experiences.

Third, **because of all the literature on dysfunctional families, there seems to be more room for parents to be human:** to acknowledge that they struggle, they fail, that they've got things they need to work on. It's safe to grow and safe to deal with those things. There is more permission for parents to work through these issues.

Fourth and finally, there are a lot more resources that are available to parents than there have been in the past.

On the negative side, one factor is **the sociological orphaning of adolescence**. Our culture tends to place adolescents into their peer groups and isolate them from significant adults, including parents, mentors, and leaders. When I work with parents and teens I find that kids are so enculturated — by the ninth grade — to not ever associate with their parents or with other adults. I know part of this is developmental, and they need that space,

Our culture turns the parent-child developmental gap into the Grand Canyon.

but **I think that our culture turns the parent-child developmental gap into a Grand Canyon. Teens really don't know how to be in a room with an adult and feel comfortable.** That is really an unfortunate outcome, but parents buy into it, too.

RH: Seems like your saying that "sociological orphaning" sounds like "relational atrophy."

RD: That's it exactly. That is a great term.

RH: There is no use of the adult-teen "relational muscle" at all.

RD: Kids can go through an entire high school career without having a significant relationship with any adult other than their youth pastor. It's not good preparation for adult maturity. Yet, it's a rampant problem. It's found in the Christian community as much as it is anywhere else.

Second, the negative media portrayal indicates that **adults are either really stupid or really confused or really screwed up.** Adults aren't going to be shown as significant people there. And yet, what I say to parents is that your teenagers' friends provide more immediate influence to their life, but parents are their most important influence. That's often not substantiated in the media, and that is really dangerous.

Third, there's this combination of being so busy, and so into material gain, and getting things done. People in my neighborhood don't just buy a house, they buy a boat. They're always gone. The idea of hanging with, being with, doing with — as a family — is lost early on. And if you don't cultivate this quality in the early years, then eventually what happens is that kids learn to get their emotional support outside the home. If you learn that, as a kid, and then you get into adolescence, you start to distance yourself from the home and you don't understand how to come back.

The fourth factor is **religious neutering in the American culture**. I think it was James Hunter who said that, previously, tolerance meant I can have my convictions and you can have yours. We can respect one another. But late 20th century tolerance means that if you have some personal convictions, then you are excluding me. A recent study in Canada found that kids are increasingly more tolerant of various views, but they're intolerant of anyone who thinks they are right. It makes it much more difficult to work towards convictions and values and how to sort those things out. **At my daughter's school some administrators made a secretary take a poinsettia out of her office because it was considered religious!** So religious beliefs are neutered, and it's not okay to be convicted about your faith.

Yet there are a significant number of people in America who are still very much interested in these religious roots. It's just that, in the media and in the pervasive culture, it is not a good thing anymore. That makes it more difficult for us, as a family. I think you are going to see a lot more of the really radical stuff, like people thinking that home schooling is the only way. A reaction to feeling out of control. I don't need to control my kids. I think parenting is not about control, it is depending upon God. That is what I do, but I have to be more intentional on how I do it, because I don't have cultural reinforcement.

Len Kageler

The rise in the influence of the media, in all of its forms, is going to continue to have a marked effect on our youth. Especially since MTV was born a decade ago, I'd say the pervasiveness of the media has increased dramatically in the lives of kids. Music has been there ever since there's been radio. But **MTV really changed all that and gave kids access to visual stuff that they didn't get**

even in movies. That's a big one. Also the Internet has, in the last couple of years, been humungously significant for kids in terms of access and influence. It's a positive thing to access educational resources that they have never in their lives dreamed of, but they're accessing a whole range of potentially destructive things also.

Josh McDowell, in his *Right from Wrong* book, says our kids are being educated in essentially a postmodern frame of mind. That means lines like: "Don't make your values normative for me," and "Just as long as you don't hurt somebody, you're fine." It's the whole relativism thing.

Dennis McCluen

Emotional deprivation in the culture is really affecting our teenagers. More people are becoming isolated. This lack of community is a very pervasive trend that affects the teen culture and their homes. Another influence would be the secularization of our culture that increasingly makes the Christian home an island. Busyness is also having a huge impact on kids and their culture.

RH: Any positives in your mind?

DM: I think that a positive is that the church has an opportunity to really do what it is called to do: build community — **to be an intergenerational resource like no other institutions in the United States today.**

Harold Ivan Smith

I see more negative at the moment. **I do not see a great era of the family coming in the future.** I see basically four key factors. Number one is violence or the fear of violence. The fear of violence is an enormous pressure concerning decision making. For example, I lead grief groups at a midcity hospital, at night. There are a lot of people who are convinced that it is in a crime area, a dangerous area, so they will not come out for programs to that area. I think a lot of people used to just tell kids, "Well, God has guardian angels to take care of you." But now we're having increased numbers of hard-to-explain deaths, and teenagers know about those incidents. It used to be parents didn't have to worry about teens who were out at night. They didn't lock their doors. All those kinds of worries that many parents grew up without having to really worry about. And now violence is an ongoing factor that they cannot easily dismiss.

The second factor is money. **This culture continues to worship money, whether they're in a church context or a nonchurch context.** We keep increasing the economic pressures on parents and on teens. We're seeing a huge growth of incredible homes, which means that the pressure on the family is to raise money to pay for the home, to pay for the cars, and all related costs that go with that. That influences family values. What does it take to live within that type of economic lifestyle? How long can we promote it before it becomes a house of cards? I'm seeing that issue with a lot of families: the pressure of what kids want and how much those objects cost.

The third factor is stress. My dad lived in another time. He pretty much knew he had a job. He didn't really worry about it too much. I don't think it really crossed his mind, yet many people raising teens these days have no guarantee of a job. Recently the merger of Boeing and Douglas was announced. They claimed that it's not going to cost jobs. Who are they trying to kid? We're talking about aerospace workers, making pretty good money. They're going to be out of jobs, and so where do they find jobs? That's stress. What do they do? They work longer hours, which means they're away from home more. As a result of that, there's a lot more stress.

When I was in China several years ago, we were talking with various people about sexuality in China. We asked them about the teenage sexuality experiences there. They laughed and said basically it doesn't exist. We found that so hard to believe, until our guide responded, "It's very simple. Where are they going to go to have privacy?" He said, **"That's your American problem. You give teenagers all this privacy, and then you are surprised that they have sex."** He said, "Where are our kids going to go? Most of them live in one-room homes or one-room apartments. There're four or five people there, members of their family: grandparents, aunts, uncles. Everybody sees everybody coming and going." That's the kind of pressure or stress that people live under.

Probably the last factor is that there's a lack of stability. You're having a family dinner and the phone rings. It's somebody wanting to clean your carpet or put siding on your house. Or a computerized call. **We are very interruptible people. The family meal, at least the evening meal, was once sacrosanct.** The standard in my day was, "Tell them you'll call them back." Now I'm not surprised when a teenager whips out a phone — like one did a couple of weeks ago — at a Sunday brunch in a very nice restaurant where I was eating. The teenager of this family decided to go along with us, and she just had a phone conversation *twice* in the middle of brunch at a table of six!

It goes back to stress and people being in a hurry. There's this lack of common courtesy, such as in the family meal. I've been trying to find the statistics that I saw in a newsletter the other day that talked about how few teenagers have meals with any sense of regularity with both parents. It just doesn't happen. **We're really a "microwave eating" culture, and it's hard to have family values around a microwave.**

> We're a "microwave eating" culture, and it's hard to have family values around a microwave.

The positive that I see is Promise Keepers. It's saying to an awful lot of men, "Your responsibilities need to be taken very, very seriously." It's equipping many through some small group, through an incredible amount of resources. If somebody could come along and develop the equivalent for wives and mothers, it could be a tandem influence that would be very, very amazing. I think that's the one positive that I see on the horizon. **I don't want to be pessimistic, but I don't see a lot of optimism in the immediate future.** I really don't see that.

Mark Cannister

On the down side, **our technological revolution is creating some problems for us.** Some leaders encourage us to pull the plug on our television sets and to save the twenty-six hours a week that the average person is spending there. But what do you replace those twenty-six hours with? What should teenagers be spending their time doing? We haven't necessarily replaced TV watching with anything constructive. **Maybe the options are even a little more destructive if teenagers are getting into some of the Internet stuff that's unhealthy.**

On the up side, **there's been a major trend of Generation X to be very service-oriented.** Yesterday, in *USA Today*, there was an article about teenagers wanting to be involved, and some teenagers even saying that they're frustrated that adults don't ask them more often to be involved in projects, ranging anywhere from Habitat For Humanity to local soup kitchens. **There seems to be a genuine motive among this generation for helping others.** And we need to capitalize on that. Maybe we haven't done a very good job, especially in the church.

Mark Senter

The concept of community, in general, has fragmented. Earlier, there was a safety net underneath people who were in stress or who had problems. Safety nets that supported people. I don't believe that those safety nets are there in such a visible way as they have been in the past. One of the reasons was the outgrowth of both the Roosevelt administration — where he tried to rescue the country through systems that he put in place, which substituted for systems that the church and local communities performed — and also "The Great Society" of Lyndon Johnson. These programs served their function for a time, but in the process the unexpected side effect was that people came to depend on these social services and quit doing the personal services they previously did.

Secondly, this shift to postmodernism set in. I find that kids do not have boundaries. Popular culture is now setting a different type of boundary for kids — boundaries based on the present. **I read in the *Chicago Tribune* this past weekend about a new school that is coming into Illinois. It has no teachers. It's modeled after an institution in New England where kids teach themselves. Of course there have always been experimental schools. Yet this new school symbolizes, for me, fragmentation — absence of any viable source of authority.**

Dan Bautista

There are three different types of teenagers I'm dealing with. One is the Latin American teenager, who is somehow limited in English, often a new immigrant. The second type is first generation Mexican-Americans. They are born of parents from Mexico or other Latin American countries. They are citizens who were born here. The third category would be the second generation teens, which we would call the Chicano population. They are 100% American. Their parents were born here, and they speak almost no Spanish at home or at school. They're all English-speaking, and they're pretty Americanized, although they come from Hispanic descent.

Racism among Hispanics is growing and also towards other non-Hispanic groups. **They're very ethnocentric. That's true of every group that we work with. They're far more materialistic than their parents, so they try to comply with the culture's expectations.**

On the positive end, there is a little more emphasis on education. I think that parents — especially those who have gone to schools — see the benefit of going to school. So there tends to be more emphasis on education, to have the kids in school. There is a big influence in our particular culture to stay away from teen parenting, or sex before marriage. It's not acceptable, even though the second generation kids are more inclined to be in that trend than the first generation Mexicans.

The other thing that is kind of unique here in the valley of South Texas is that teenagers tend to be more sympathetic to the

needs of others, perhaps because parents came from poor surroundings, or because many of them are still experiencing poverty. They tend to be more sensitive to social issues, in terms of poverty and the things that poverty brings, like dependency on government and low morale.

RH: How do they express that sympathy?

DB: They want to help nongovernment agencies that are helping the poor. We have teenagers right now in every high school that have been doing Christmas programs for the poor in different colonies. There are about 100 different colonies in the valley. So, they're also doing more projects like Habitat for Humanity, building houses for the poor. **They tend to share more easily with others.**

Jay Kesler

I've done a lot of lecturing on this topic and I start with the major shift, from naturalism to supernaturalism. Our grandparents were pretty much raised in an atmosphere where science reigned, where the world was looking at a post-Christian period, scientifically. A postsupernatural period, because liberalism in the church was running rampant; the Bible was under question, and so on. With the mind-altering drugs and other kinds of experiences of the '60s, we had a different kind of supernaturalism on our hands, whereby old-fashioned liberalism and modernism were no longer there. We were left with a strange form of supernaturalism. You had the occult, Eastern religions, and other drug-oriented experiences.

We used to argue between faith and unbelief; that is, if you were a Christian you believed that God intervened in human history, the virgin birth, and that God made the sun stand still. Now everybody believes in all kinds of strange and unscientific things. They believe in things that go bump in the night. So, Christianity finds itself with this present group of young people, battling for which form of supernaturalism has the most appeal. Or, for which is the most strange, or the one that affects your life more. You have all the New Age stuff and the television advertising psychic hot lines, for example.

We have almost the opposite problem we had with our parents and grandparents. Then, we were trying to say that there is such a thing as supernaturalism. Now we're trying to put some kind of bounds on supernaturalism, with doctrine. We're trying to say that there's Christian faith. Yes, this is supernaturalistic faith, but it has bounds to it. There are boundaries in the New Testament doctrine. So that, to me, is a major issue that kids are struggling with. The appeal is to some of these more bizarre forms of supernaturalism — their claims are so much more extreme than the claims of the Christian faith. They're especially attractive to impressionable young people; they provide a tremendous pull. Kids are unduly fascinated with Satan, unduly fascinated with the occult. Then, add to this cinematography, which has become so clever. Kids regularly see strange stuff happening before their very eyes. We also have a group of kids that are really confused about the natural world and where supernaturalism enters in.

The second thing I talk about in relationship to trends is narcissism, the whole idea of starting with myself as the center of the universe, as opposed to God being the center. That which makes me happy, that which gives me pleasure is good. Anything that brings me inconvenience or pain is bad. Now the Christian message, in its orthodox form, tells us that we live in a world where we experience pain. But kids are told by this culture that you don't have to experience pain; there is some kind of a bromide to help you escape all of that. The Christian message calls for sacrifice and duty, topics less attractive to them. There is tremendous preoccupation with the self. **Whereas a former generation understood that man's relationship with God was obedience and duty, today it's reversed: God is to do something for us, to take away our pain.** About seven out of the ten books you see in Christian bookstores are of what I call the "Christian psychological genre," trying to convince people that if you push God's buttons you can get a world where everything comes up roses. This is a really great perversion of the Incarnational principle, but it's huge in kid's minds. We even have Christians attempting to accommodate this perverted Christian gospel, like these "name it and claim it" preachers. It removes the

Cross from the Christian message. A neighborhood kid gets leukemia, but your kid gets a pony, if you pray. It negates the Christian faith.

Some say this present group of kids is like the 1950's generation: both are apathetic. But we were apathetic in the '50s because we were ignorant of the world. We didn't know about the world. We felt we'd paid our dues in the Second World War; we didn't care about the world. **These kids know a great deal about the world, and they care a great deal. Their problem is they think they don't matter. These kids have a great identity crisis. They don't see how they could possibly change the world. So they're struggling with self-esteem.** By the way, I think that the Christians who are critical of the self-esteem movement have a point, but they also miss a point. And the point they miss is that unless a person senses he or she is a unique creation of God — that "if God be for us, who can be against us" — unless they have some sense of identity like that, then they are made impotent. They simply sit on their hands and watch the world go by. It's not unlike shell shock, I think. The media has so filled their minds with the world's problems that they don't see how one little person could possibly change it. So, people say they're apathetic, and I say, "Yeah, they may be apathetic, but I think that we've assigned to young people tasks that the world has never solved, and we should be careful not to do them in." Their circuits are overloaded.

Then, of course, I try to establish the fact that **we are facing a tremendously distorted view of love, commitment, and sex. Sex has become an appetite, like hunger. You have sex to get love.** Making love has become the same as sexuality. This has become very confusing for these kids. With such tremendous insecurity, the ideological plates of the earth are shifting on them. Kids really have a hard time understanding the Christian view of sexuality. Things that we would call trust, fidelity, and duty — the kinds of things that their grandparents attach to love and marriage — they see these as more of a passing thing. Sex is like hunger. You satisfy it, then go on to something else. It's not a cement that holds male and female together over a period of time. **They're really afraid of commitment. Kids are really**

afraid of giving themselves to another person for fear that they will be disappointed, because they've seen it with their parents, and their classmates. When I was in my elementary class, only one kid was from a divorced home. Now, 5 to 7 out of 10 kids in the class have some kind of a disjuncture.

Finally, I discuss socioeconomic realities, like this being the first generation that is going to settle for less than their parents. We're developing a permanent underclass in this country — tremendous distance between the rich and the poor. And shrinking the middle class. Many people look at teenage angst, and they see these problems as a leading cause of teenage suicide. I think it is there, but I think that spiritual emptiness is the larger cause of suicide.

Chapter 2
Roadblocks & Bridges

When you focus on the teen and their family life, what "roadblocks" (to put it negatively) and what "bridges" (to state it positively) do you typically see today?

Thom Schultz

I sense a degree of selfishness from many parents that manifests itself in a lot of different ways. Parents have found it fashionable to say things like, "I'm not fulfilled" or "'I've got to do what is right for me." It's a selfish cry to the pressures that they feel, and it's leaving victims along the way, mainly the kids. **Parental selfishness has cropped up curiously, in another way, by parents living vicariously through their kids.** That has always been there to a certain degree, but the intensity of our busy, contemporary life has just magnified it. Trying to live their lives vicariously through their kids' sports activities, academics, and career plans. You see it with a recent controversial incident in the news: the little girl beauty pageants!

Mike Yaconelli

Busyness is the number one roadblock. Families are incredibly busy. They encourage it and are proud of it. They see it as a

sign of worth. And that makes sense because, in a society where you personally don't matter — where there is no personal meaning — if you run around and keep busy, then you must be meaningful.

Ron Habermas: Things like church functions and clubs and sports.

MY: Yes, church is full of activity. Parents' lives are full of activity. They encourage their kids to get involved in sports and all that kind of thing.

The second roadblock is an acceptance of cultural values. It's more than just an intellectual thing. It's seeped into our being. So, the difference between now and twenty years ago is that all of these things that we were talking about then are now real and part of our lives.

RH: So, busyness and acceptance of cultural values are problems.

MY: Yes, more than just intellectual acceptance, but a real, genuine . . .

RH: Ownership?

MY: Yeah. For example, parents are concerned that their children get a very good education. Why? So they can spend forty thousand dollars to get a degree they won't use? **Most of these kids don't have a clue as to what they want to do with their lives. They've never heard anyone talk about giftedness or calling. That's what the church is about — we believe in calling. So really, we ought not to be sending kids to college, most of them, after high school. Rather, we ought to be sending them to Africa and India and someplace in the world where they can make a difference, and discover what their gifts are. Then decide on whether or not they want to go to school.** Because we don't really care whether or not a kid gets high SATs or unbelievable grades. When they're ready to learn, and when they're ready to really immerse themselves in what their gifts are and how to make those gifts better, then they'll go to school. They'll be motivated. They'll learn. That's why we don't want 50-year-olds coming in our college class, because they ask too many questions. They want to do longer term papers. They get them in early. Because they're motivated. But you see what happens if you, as a youth worker, say to the kids, "You don't need to go to college. Don't worry about it." You're fired. You're gone.

Let's take sports. **Sports today is nothing but treating people like they're a piece of meat. Why would we be supportive of this? Why would we want our children to do that? The whole worship of being number one, being successful, and being at the top is just the most incredible and unbelievable thing. Why? We shouldn't believe in that.** We believe in being last, little, lost. But we have totally bought into that cultural value. And not only have we bought into it, we believe that Jesus and the youth group and church are all there to make that all happen — and that God, of course, would want that to happen, because that's what really matters.

> Sports today is nothing but treating people like they're a piece of meat. Why would we be supportive of this?

Les Parrott

One of the roadblocks I've seen is the apathy that comes from the adolescents' relationships with their moms and dads. The majority of homes that teenagers are growing up in are fractured, so the relationships aren't much to speak of. **Apathy comes from seeing fracturedness — that Mom and Dad can't hold their own relationship together.** It comes from feeling racial tensions; it comes from feeling there are environmental issues that offer no quick solutions. Seeing financial problems at the national level. **This generation basically feels like they got ripped off. America's best years are over. The best families are over, and they don't get much. Therefore, they're left with apathy.**

> This generation basically feels like they got ripped off. America's best years are over.

Helen Musick

I agree that one of the roadblocks is apathy, and that's basically seen in a parent feeling, "I can't make a difference." There are too many external pressures; negative things that cause that thinking. Also, **our culture breeds isolation** — everything from the amount of TV, to the computer and the Internet. How much energy and attention that takes up, not just for the kids, but parents, too.

Another roadblock would combine time and possessions. There's such a demand upon everybody to do everything. And there are the monetary demands: the need "to have."

Finally, there's a roadblock of the absence of the traditional, cooperative mission of raising kids in the local community. Everyone pitching in to raise teens. Something like the incident I had with my child. A neighbor child, age six, was basically talking about pornographic movies to my five year old. Well, as I confronted the parent, I became her enemy. I guess her argument was, because it was going on in their home, it was none of my business. That was one example. Here's another: I was driving down our neighborhood street the other day, and a car raced past me going 75 mph. I thought maybe there was an emergency, so I followed the car to where it was going to see if I could help. Out jumps a teenage girl just leisurely going into her house. Then I was confronted with, "Well, I don't know these people," but do I look up in our residential directory, find out whose home it was, call the parents, and let them know? Maybe they'll think I'm invading their privacy, or they'll cuss me out. But I chose to say, if it was my kid, I would want someone to take a mutual role in raising my child and say, "This is not right. I saw your child doing this. For her sake and others, you need to talk to her." That's what I'm talking about. There's an absence of community support.

RH: How did that go, when you talked to those parents?

HM: It went okay, actually. When I looked up their name, I knew who they were. They probably didn't know who I was, but the father is a Christian psychiatrist. And the mother said, "Yes, the kids are all in a big hurry, and I'm glad that you brought that to our attention." **But there was still fear in me, in that I didn't know what to expect. I don't think that was true just a few years ago.**

David Olshine

I did a parents' seminar just yesterday in a church and, as I'm talking to these people, I'm looking at many of them right in their eyes. I'm seeing heads nodding. I'm seeing many of them laughing in response to the things we're talking about. So I'm excited to see that some parents really are interested in connecting with their kid. Yet, for others — I'm looking into their eyes, too — and I'm seeing blank stares. I see no emotions. **I'm seeing some parents who are clueless. Maybe they don't give their kids much time at all. They don't know their kids. They don't know their kids' world. They've lost touch with who they are.** Not only have they lost touch with their own adolescence (who they used to be), but they don't have a clue who they are now. And when you don't have a clue who you are, you're not going to want to invest your life in anybody. **So I think the main roadblock I'm seeing is apathy. A lot of parents just don't really give a rip. They say they do, but their body language and their actions prove otherwise.**

RH: Any positive bridges that you see?

DO: There are some parents that have decided that they are going to start parenting when their kids are young. There are two families that I know that intentionally don't have TVs. I've asked them why, and one family said, "We don't even have the time to watch TV." They spend a lot of time in communication with their kids. That's very encouraging.

Ginny Olson

Parents have a sense of fear. Fear like "I can't be too nosy; I can't be too strict; I don't want my kid to think that I'm not cool, because I promised myself that I would never be like my parents." Consequently, parents are afraid of enforcing boundaries. Yet these kids are saying, "Give me boundaries. Yes, I'm going to push against them."

RH: How do you see kids asking for boundaries? What are some indicators?

GO: Good question. **I've seen it in small groups where teens will push against the authority. They actually told the adult, "Give us rules. You're the adult here." It provides a sense of safety for them.** In passing conversations with peers, where they like to rag on their parents, there's a sense of safety if they know, "Okay, my parents care enough that I have to be home at this curfew time, that I can't do this, and that I can't hang out with a certain kind of people."

Harold Ivan Smith

One of the roadblocks I see is, again, the stress which filters down. When I was growing up you'd hear, "Don't bother your father, he's reading the paper. He's taking a nap." Now we just don't bother our fathers, period. There are parents who are home, but aren't "home" when they're home, because the phone can interrupt at any hour, they've got work to do, or their mind is not there. They may be sitting there in the den watching TV — they are physically present — but they're not really emotionally present. That's one of the prominent blocks.

> I call it the "Sally Jessie Raphael Syndrome," which means that, some way, I'm going to mess up my kid, as a parent.

There's also something I call the "Sally Jessie Raphael Syndrome," which is that "some way, I'm going to mess up my kid." I'm going to end up seeing them on *Sally Jessie Raphael* someday, telling me what a horrible parent — telling the world what a horrible parent — I was. There is that fear that my child is not going to turn out right. That my dreams for my child are not going to be reached. It's that pressure to be a great parent that is another really prominent roadblock. **What I have told parents, especially single parents, is to be a "good enough" parent. If you're trying to be *the* world's greatest parent, you're setting yourself up for a lot of**

pain. But if you'll concentrate on being a good parent, a solid parent, a parent who's there, I think that's extremely important.

Mark Cannister

The biggest barrier is understanding the culture. If parents don't understand the culture that teens are growing up in, they're going to have a real hard time understanding their own teenagers. Maybe you can even back up and say that **parents need to understand that their teens live in a different culture.** It's more than simply a *generation gap.* There's a real *cultural gap.* There's a different culture.

Parents need to prepare to work with their teenagers, in the same way that they would prepare to work with a culturally-diverse group of people, as missionaries. As one example — probably the biggest example — **parents need to know the music of their teenagers.** They need to listen to it. They need to talk to their teenagers about it. They need to understand it. They need to see some of their videos. They need to read *Rolling Stone.* They need to understand the whole music scene because music is such a large part of teenagers' lives.

The bridge that I'm trying to create is a bridge of communication. You can't communicate with somebody if you don't know their language, their customs, or culture. I think parents need to be more proactive in gaining that understanding.

Dennis McCluen

The first road block that inhibits parents of youth is parents themselves. We are basically a self-centered culture. Parenting presses that issue more than anything else in our lives. A huge roadblock is that we remain self-oriented. Many choices that I see parents making are about the parents' selfish desires that directly affect the next generations. The second part of that would be self-doubt. **A lot of parents don't know what to do, or they think they are not very good at parenting.** They have doubts about themselves, their parenting and their training.

Len Kageler

Let's start with bridges. One is that Baby Boomer parents are more communicative than their parents were. They are more able, generally, to talk about feelings, to be "real," to not just suffer in silence or to deal with things by withdrawal. I think our parents often tended to deal with stress by withdrawal and violence.

The negative thing would be that most Baby Boomer parents have been out of touch with youth culture. They came of age in the late '60s and '70s, and now that their kids are coming of age, they don't know what's normal. And that really causes confusion and distress among parents.

RH: What do you mean — what's "normal" among youth culture?

LK: What is normal youth behavior, how kids act, and how they think. My suggestion is to get more on the proactive side: **Parents need to volunteer in a ministry of their church when their kid is in fourth or fifth grade. That experience will help them tremendously to know what to expect when their child becomes a teen.**

Rick Dunn

The number one hurdle for parents to deal with is their own family origin and background. One of my youth ministry students got his girlfriend pregnant. She didn't want to marry him. She was about to start another relationship and he didn't know what to do. It was crazy. He asked me if I would sit down and meet with his parents and help him. So his parents came to meet with me and the first fifteen minutes we just talked. (I'll call the young man John). Then his dad started saying, "Well, John has got to do this and this," and his mom said, "You're always doing that to him." Now that's fifteen minutes into the conversation. Five minutes later, I am guiding them towards the dynamic of their own relationship, by discovering that Dad always comes down hard and Mom always compensates by going easy. Ten minutes later, Dad is talking about his own family. His father was emotionally distant from him, and he has never figured out how to connect with John. Now we're dealing with Dad's and Mom's differences (in their own families) and how that affected the way they are parenting. So the primary issue is not really what they should get John to do. It's how they can work together in their marriage so that they can have the resources John needs to get through. I find that scenario over and over again.

Adolescents push every identity issue that we personally have, as parents. And our role is always changing. If we parents are not sure if we are needed or what we are supposed to do, those unresolved things out of our own past can emerge. And if a parent is not aware of those factors and he or she is not working on those, they can be very trapped by them. Either by doing that which their parents did — which may not be productive — or overreacting to the past and trying not to be like their parents.

A second influence is the magnetic pull of the youth culture. It's often just parents backing off, but there is a strong pull for kids to move away from the home and be active in their youth culture. Consider their clothing, music, and activities. There is a whole range of issues for an adolescent in youth culture. **If you want to keep the strong influence on your teen, you have to keep your relationship with them strong. I'm not sure parents know how to do that.**

And the third factor is the misconception about adolescent experiences. Most parents don't really understand the adolescent experience in this culture. The norms and the expectations that parents grew up with are easy to project onto these kids. And when they don't work, parents feel at a loss about what to do. **For instance, asking a kid to be a godly young man or young woman in this culture is like asking them to swim upstream.** That's a different scenario than what some of us grew up with.

Wayne Rice

Parents fear their children becoming teenagers. There's a dread that many parents feel about having teenagers in their home. **It becomes self-fulfilling prophecy. If you expect kids to become problems when they turn into teenagers, that's what you get.**

People tend to live up to or down to expectations we have. **As adults, we don't associate very much with teenagers, so they're like foreigners. We don't know what to expect.**

> Parents have no inherent sense of "I can do this." They're confused.

Which brings up another roadblock, and that's just a lack of confidence. **Parents have no inherent sense of "I can do this." They're confused. They don't know what to do. They're like, "Someone help me, I have no idea how to relate to this kid. She's driving me crazy."** But really we don't associate much with teenagers. They're isolated from us.

It's a whole different culture. Teenagers have always been seeking an identity separated from their parents. That's typical of kids for thousands of years. But now, the whole culture has separated from the adult culture. **What happens when you have an alien culture is that communication breaks down. They speak a different language.** They communicate in totally different ways. They have secrets you don't know about. There's a whole breakdown which is caused by adult abandonment. **To illustrate, I have a hard time if I go into the inner city — where there's a whole section of town that's Vietnamese — and I can't even read their signs. Similarly, a lot of parents have no idea what language is being spoken by their kids because they're just not part of it.**

Roger Cross

Let me start with the roadblocks. One is the time pressure for parents. We live in such a fast-paced society. My family is a good example of that problem. And any parent — but particularly a Christian parent — has to really fight against that factor. **If we allow ourselves to be swept along by the culture, trying to do everything that the culture is doing, that's one of the biggest roadblocks. The family is like any other relationship. The family blossoms in time — time spent with one another. What's bidding for their time — that's their biggest enemy.**

RH: I hear you saying two things. They're too busy, and secondly, they're too busy with the wrong things.

RC: Right. It's not that they've necessarily made bad choices. It's just that the society puts multiple pressures on parents and teens. Pressures to have certain things, which require significant time on their job. The pressure of all that takes them away from spending time in the right places.

Mark Senter

The confidence of parents has eroded enormously. Tony Campolo pointed out that a long time ago parents just sort of lived their own lives and let the kids raise the kids, so to speak. There was an entire social system built into this model, which was mainly rural. **Now we're told that your kid has to be your best friend. That, in turn, brings a new level of unrealistic expectation and anxiety. And there's a lack of confidence. I don't want to go to the other extreme and say authoritarianism is needed, but there is a confidence that's needed to be a parent. The "calling to parenthood," for Christian families, is something that should be explored and developed.**

RH: What would that mean to you — a "calling for Christian parenting"?

MS: The fact is that my success is not judged by how my kids turn out. Success comes from God, who made me, gave me the capacity to be a parent, and allowed me to be a parent. When there's a parent-teen struggle, you need to be very careful when you go back and say, "Where did we go wrong?" **It's not enough to come up with just theological answers at an emotional time of struggle,** but that does help. If I didn't have some answers, it would be even more devastating.

> My success is not judged by how my kids turn out.

Haman Cross

I fear that parents will manipulate technology so it will help them. Instead of them teaching a kid about e-mail or the Internet, they will rely on technology. **Technology tells them that they don't need to perform the duties of a parent; it can be the substitute. I see technology making it more convenient for parents, but not really helping them to parent.** Nowadays you can do everything you do by the Internet: communication, sex, war. You name it. Rather I'd like to see parents who say, "Let's see if we can sanctify technology and use it for good purposes." Which we can and we should.

RH: What's missing? What can technology not do that parents need to do?

HC: Technology can't replace the human talk, touch, and the power of presence. Parents don't need to just say something, but they need to be there. To experience the child's frustrations, tears, and joy. To chat on the Internet is nothing like being there in person. **Let me use an analogy: Technology is like God being "up there" in the heavens; it's quite another thing for Him to be Emmanuel — "with us." That absent parent misses the developmental years, loses the opportunity to bond, to understand, and to watch their kids.**

Ken Davis

The roadblock of the materialistic philosophy we have in our country. That providing for your family means having a certain kind of home, driving a certain number of cars — or a certain kind of car — and establishing a certain lifestyle. **We have lost track of the quality of the home for our children. Actually, it's much more important to focus on *who* we are than *what* we have.** As a result, parents are driven to hold down two jobs, so that they can maintain the lifestyle that they feel is necessary for the home. That wouldn't be necessary if we weren't so materialistic.

Also, our culture has a great inhibiting factor on parents with youth. It used to be that there was an anticipation among

teenagers and adults — what we used to call the "generation gap." Kids expected to lose communication with their parents, because that's what the culture demanded. You no longer talked with your parents; you weren't to be seen with your parents; you didn't go places with your parents.

Now, that relationship has gotten even more perverted — and that's probably a good word — by what is shown on MTV. You not only lose communication with your parents, but outright rebellion is considered the chic, "in thing" to do. You don't listen to your parents. Your parents are a nonentity in the home.

It's a reflection of what we've also chosen to do with God. **God is a nonentity. It's not that He's bad or good, or doesn't exist. It's a no-brainer; He just doesn't count. That's what our culture is teaching parents and teens.**

> God is a nonentity. It's not that He's bad or good, or doesn't exist. He just doesn't count. That's what our culture is teaching parents and teens.

Marlene LeFever

Most of the parents of teenagers today are still Boomers, but they're young Boomers, so they're a bridge generation between the older Gen Xers, and the younger Boomers. They take on some of the characteristics of both groups: Negatively this means that we've got some problems with fathering. So one of the bridges that needs to be reinforced is educating the generation that is parenting on what it means to parent. (This is true of mothers as well.) **Fifty percent of the parenting group right now grew up, for some part of their lives — from ages birth to 18 — in a single parent family. For many of them, that was a female-dominated family. So how do they father their children? And, as Christians, we ask: "What do you do with the concept of God as Heavenly Father?"** That's one area where we need to create an educational bridge.

Another area may be the identification of life passages: for kids to see themselves growing up — with healthy family traditions — where there are markers along their way for them to celebrate. **We need to build celebration into families.** I'm not sure that is something unique to this generation, but it's unique to the American culture. Not celebrations like Christmas, but events that are momentous to an individual family, like getting on the honor roll, a girl's first period, and getting a driver's license. **Celebrate what it means to be an adult.** And I think that celebration will be different in each home. **As far as for the church, I think we should begin to celebrate the passage from fifth grade to sixth grade — the middle school passage.** Many churches are just ignoring the fact that school systems are now built on middle school, and they still have junior high and senior high school ministries. And we need to celebrate the end of childhood.

> Take away the whole idea of Christianity being easy, and put some teeth into it.

Take away the whole idea of Christianity being easy, and put some teeth into it. Public school is doing this with these kids, and why in the world shouldn't our Christian education patterns as well?

I think also we need, as a church, to affirm the things that this generation can do that the church doesn't know how to do. Things like building a new program for the computer, structuring devotions for your peers through the Internet, all sorts of terminologies and wonders that I don't even know how to talk about — let alone do — and these kids can do it. They dream it, and not only can they dream it (because the Boomers could dream it), they can put it into practice. **I think the church should celebrate what *teens* can do that the senior pastor can't.**

Dave Rahn

Unless parents are very clear-minded about their vision for parenting, by default all sorts of influences take place just

because of our culture. For example, schools are more demanding in every single extra-curricular activity in which they involve kids. If they choose to be involved, teens don't commit to just practice. It's also selling things. It's being involved in summers — sometimes year-round commitments — whether in sports or drama or student government. They become life commitments for teens. You have to be clear-minded to sometimes resist those influences in culture and say, **"Wait a minute; among the things that are vying for my kid's time, the family needs to be a contender."** I think that one of the other contributors — not so much on the kid's side, but on the parents' — is the increase in both parents working outside the home. **If parents are increasingly busy, that makes them increasingly unreflective about their parenting responsibility.**

Dan Bautista

The roadblocks include materialism. Both parents tend to work. They get very involved in work, and this cuts down the time that they are spending with their kids. The parents are struggling with the tradeoffs between parenting from the ways of the old generation and that of the new generation.

Also, communication is not very good sometimes. That's one of the things that teenagers have expressed. They want parents to be able to talk to them without always giving them instructions, or scolding them, or telling them what they have done wrong. Just talk to them. And there's plenty more information available on parenting than there used to be. Kids are reading more materials about how to communicate better; how to prepare better for the future. **For example, one of the popular resources in the churches here are novels. Christian teenage novels. Within the novels are some hidden messages about respect,** which is a big issue in our culture: "respecto."

RH: Which novels in particular?

DB: Some teen books from Focus on the Family. We also have some new literature about Hispanic settlers and adventures of Spanish conquistadors. Not all resources are Christian, yet most

61

focus on dignity and respect. For example, the nuclear family is the center of their plot and attention.

Jay Kesler

The ground shift over personal rights is bigger than most people think it is. Children's rights versus parental rights. The former generation thought of life in terms of parents being in charge, having authority, and didn't think to question it. Courts backed it up; schools backed it up. Now, kids have an overemphasis on individual rights. Kids are taught to question all authority — their parents, the schools, whatever. You have teachers who are afraid to discipline for fear they will be accused of some sort of abuse. Parents are afraid to discipline for fear that they are doing something wrong, and that they will be dragged into the courtroom. Especially among the more rebellious youth, you'll find that kids will play this card rather quickly — very quickly — on adults. **This shift in authority is a huge, huge factor.** And there are court cases, every day, where there are terrible illustrations of misuse of parental power, so that gives this trend just enough legitimacy.

> The ground shift over personal rights is bigger than most people think it is.

I do an interesting exercise with a group of kids when I speak to them. I say "Tell me your grandparents' story — their favorite lines." They'll immediately throw out clichés like, "Can't tell a book by its cover" and "Hard work is important." They'll refer to the Depression, the Second World War, patriotism, and the flag. Then I say, "Tell me your parents' story," and they get really quiet. They don't say anything. I find that the parents — in their kids' minds — are ambivalent. As I try to think why, I realize that their parents were raised during the sexual revolution. Those parents obviously are not wanting to be hypocritical, so they're not so sure what to say to their kids. **Their grandparents have no trouble saying, "All drugs are wrong," and, "Teenagers shouldn't drink." They spoke** in declarative sentences; **these kids don't hear declarative sentences from their parents. They're confused.** I think there is a certain nobility about not wanting to be a hypocrite; the parents don't want to tell teens not to do something that they did. But, by the same token, **these kids many times identify much more with their grandparents than with their parents. Because their grandparents are forthright. And teens feel like their grandparents know where they are at.**

Leith Anderson

Parents have — themselves — increasingly come from dysfunctional families. Mothers and fathers have come from different families of origin, in terms of the models they have grown up with. They're coming with discrepancy in terms of their own knowledge of parenting. Many times, *they* were not well parented, so *they* don't know how to parent. That becomes a significant issue on how they approach their children. There needs to be — at least we're perceiving that there needs to be — a whole lot of information available to help these parents of teenagers.

RH: Okay, so there's an information gap. What other kinds of strategies does the church need to employ besides simply more good information?

LA: There is, in our culture, a deep-seated belief that **the**

> The generations are growing increasingly shorter. If you had teenagers five years ago, you really don't know how to parent teenagers today, because the situation has changed so dramatically.

generations are growing increasingly shorter. If you had teenagers five years ago, you really don't know how to parent teenagers today, because the situation has changed so dramatically. I'm not sure whether that's true, but it is certainly perceived to be true. **There's a sense in which the very people who can mentor are discredited.** That's certainly the perception. A simple example is the use of marijuana. There are a lot of Baby Boomers who themselves used marijuana, and they came out okay. But now they are repeatedly being told that the purity and the strength of the marijuana that's on the street today is much more potent than what they had when they were in their years of experimentation. They really have a dilemma, because they did it, but they're telling their kids not to do it. That's, at least, an example of our changing culture and its problems.

Chapter 3
Advice for All Caregivers

What's one piece of advice you wish you could give to every parent? What's one insight that all need to hear?

Ken Davis

I would quote a friend of mine, Zig Ziglar: "Love is spelled 'time.'" The ability to set down what you are doing, look your child in the eye, and give them your full attention. When they're talking to you — and I believe that communication patterns are established in preschool years — each child learns how important their relationship is to their parents.

Ron Habermas: So, those formative years are pretty critical.

KD: That's when they subconsciously and consciously pick up the cues for what it's all about. **In those early years they need to have heard the words, "I love you," hundreds and hundreds of times. They need to have seen that love is unconditional, that it is not withheld for either bad behavior or bad grades or nonperformance or whatever.** That doesn't mean that there's no discipline in the home. But those are the years when they need to know that, when they talk to their mom or dad, their parents won't be watching TV and trying to carry on a conversation at the same time. Or reading a newspaper and grunting an answer, instead of paying full attention.

Hold your children, touch your children — all through life.

The other thing I would say is to hold your children, touch your children — all through life. We had a woman at our workshop who began to give a speech and couldn't continue it. Her father had adored her, but when she reached puberty — because touching is such a sexually-oriented thing in our society — her father abandoned her. He no longer touched her. He no longer hugged her. He no longer kissed her, or anything. His motivations may have been well intended, but he left a woman who is now in her forties — and very successful — with a huge, empty gap in her life where she needed her father the most. So, I would say, that **although love is spelled "t-i-m-e," we need to say the words. We need to touch our children. And then, probably the most important one of all, we must model for our children a solid, growing relationship with Christ that impacts our behavior. That means more than just going to church. It means more than just having family devotions. It means that kids see their parents change, as a result of their own faith.**

Leith Anderson

I think what parents most need is information and peer relationships. Because today's parents of teenagers are typically acting within isolation. They don't know what's normal; they don't know what's abnormal. They don't know what to do. They don't know what's healthy; they don't know what's unhealthy.

RH: So it's necessary information, but it's also processing it with colleagues, with peers.

LA: Yes, ideally with healthy peers. **One of the biggest revelations to many people who are struggling with raising their teenage children is to discover that other parents deal with the exact same issues they have. They're surprised by that.**

RH: So, finding common ground — the fact that they're not unique — is advantageous?

LA: Oh, yes. **Others have survived and they'll survive as well.**

One of the biggest revelations to many parents who are struggling is to discover that other parents deal with the exact same issues.

Les Parrott

First, don't assume that your son or daughter has the same set of needs that you had when you were in their shoes. Parents must realize that the youth culture today is very different than it was for them. **In other words, if I could give parents a gift, it would be the gift of empathy. That capacity to put themselves in their kid's shoes and really see the world from their perspective.** That's the foundational message that I would want to present to them.

The second thing that I would try to convey is that their kids don't need any more advice or any more answers. They need relationships. They need a relationship with Mom and Dad. To do that, Mom and Dad don't need to be like teenagers, they need to be like parents. Those are the two primary messages.

Jay Kesler

The most important advice to give to young parents who are raising small children is that they raise children intentionally and in an atmosphere of love, discipline, and clear messages of consistent behavior. That's the place to start — with small children. The real tension is in the lives of teenagers, where the parents *didn't* do these things when the kids were young. Now they're trying to build, putting a basement under a house — after it's already built. You can do that, but it's a lot of work. I see that requiring great forthrightness on the part of the parents. A certain level of vulnerability, where the parents are willing to say, "Son, I know I missed it. I know I wasn't saying these things earlier, but my faith has become more clear now. I'm more aware of who I am, as your parent, and I'm asserting myself in these areas because I love you and I'm concerned for you." **In other words, I think it takes more communication on the part the parent — more vulnerability — when you find out that you've neglected this parental task until they're about fifteen.** And I think there are an awful lot of examples like that out there.

I *don't* think it's going to be there so much in the next generation. I am extremely pleased by what I see in the churches: the numbers of parenting conferences and the way the young couples get together and talk about their responsibilities. And I also am happy to see more male involvement in family. You know, if a baby cries in a church today, 70 percent of the time the dad will take the baby out. Thirty years ago if a baby cried, the mother would always take the baby out. I think these trends are very positive. I think the church has responded to much of this crisis. They've responded beautifully to this need, but it's going to take a little time to turn this around. It's like turning the *Queen Mary*. It's going to take a lot of time. Now, I'm speaking here of the evangelical subculture. I think the larger culture is up for grabs, because the parents are also in rebellion against God. They are not interested in these same values. They're interested in their rights, in libertarian behaviors, and so they're raising their kids in an indifferent fashion. **We're developing two cultures in this country side by side. That's very frightening.**

RH: Is that going to lead to some eventual conflict, in your mind?

JK: **I think the conflict will take place over the responsible people getting tired of paying the bills for the irresponsible. We've got it now, for instance, in the areas of AIDS and welfare. I mean, why should I pay a premium for my automobile insurance because somebody insists on being drunk? Or why should I pay a premium for my health insurance when people insist on smoking cigarettes?** Why should I pay a premium on my life insurance because somebody insists on irresponsible homosexual behavior? But then the law says that we can't discriminate by having preferential treatment, like nonsmokers insurance. Of course this will cause one group to pay everything and the other to pay nothing or a smaller amount.

So, as they force us all into larger groups, I think there will be tensions like culture wars going on. I predict this will happen. Same thing is true in the school systems. We are seeing a great exodus out of the public schools, not just by Christians. I used to think that home schooling was a phenomenon only among evangelicals. It's not. It's among people who simply do not want to pay taxes and then have their children in the schools where they are learning nothing. So, the responsible side of culture is getting weary of the weight of the irresponsible side. What in the world will happen when we divide them, I don't know. Can we even end up living in the same country?

Mark Senter

Laugh a lot. Don't be afraid to celebrate. Those are two different facets of the same diamond. We should laugh at ourselves as parents, at our mistakes. Though we have a calling to parenthood, we're imperfect people. And laughing with our kids is a source of solidarity. Celebration — and also establishing traditions built around the church — are very, very important. Sociologists suggest that one of the great indicators of family solidarity is traditions. We must have those rich traditions, whether they are what you do on Christmas morning, or Thanksgiving, or Saturday morning, or Sunday evening. Establishing traditions becomes a part of the celebration of life. They don't need to be a drudgery. They can add a buoyancy and laughter to family life.

> Laugh a lot. Don't be afraid to celebrate.

Dave Rahn

None of my answers are easy ones. They are all costly to parents. There is an urgent need for parents to carve out space where they can be intentional in the leadership of their family. That will require good reflection, evaluation on a regular basis, and discipline in that direction. That probably was the single most important strategy for Christian families in the past. It's like what we ask the leaders of the church to do: to step back and reflect on what's going on, what needs to happen, and what I have to do to make that happen. As parents we must similarly ask: **Do my children have the power to make the decisions that are best for their health right now, or do I have to step in and — by imposing discipline or adding encouragement — help them out?** That's my number one strategy that impacts others. And it opens up other strategies.

RH: So there's a need for more sophisticated reflection on parent leadership. What are one or two other questions a parent would ask if they were to take this advice seriously?

DR: The first question would be to ask of each member of the family what character "fruit" is being observed in the home? What kind of people are we becoming? There are all sorts of spin-off questions: When we're tired, what are we like? Are we tired most of the time? What are we like under stress? Are we under stress most of the time? How do we treat other people? Do we have time for other people?

RH: What else would test the pulse beat of the family?

DR: The next category is the relationship questions between members of the family. If there are two kids and two parents, you've got several combinations of relationships. Once you assess those relationships, you ask yourself: Is there anything I can do to help that relationship along? **If, in my assessment, I discover that my kids are not learning to like each other but to dislike each other, I begin to think — intentionally — what am I going to do?** Do the current behavior patterns in our home contribute to that end? Is there anything that I can impose that's going to carefully confront or encourage different behavior?

Roger Cross

Most parents realize the problem too late, and they try to correct it when their kids are teenagers. But I do see some better teaching on this topic, right now, in the family and in the church. I do see a shift (I don't have any statistics to document this) with Christian parents trying very hard to make sure that one of them is at home when their kids are young. So there is a flicker of hope there for me. Parents are saying, "If we're going to tackle this thing, we have to do it when the kids are young." For example, kids get to the teenage years. Mom and Dad are just sitting there at the dinner table — when they realize that their kids haven't been there for a week — and they're saying, "What do we do?"

And I'm not even sure that time with your kids when they become teenagers is quite that important. It's much more important when they're younger. You still have to adjust to youth; you have to learn to know their schedules. But it's a different kind of time than when they're young.

RH: So, could I synthesize your comments into one line of advice to say, "Hey parents, one of you needs to be staying at home"?

RC: Particularly when their kids are young. I'd say, "Parents, spend time with your kids when they're younger, recognizing that those are your most influential years. It's what's going to show when they're older."

RH: So youth ministry starts in preschool?

RC: Absolutely. **I've often seen parents try to deal with issues related to their teenagers, but those same issues go way back to when the kids were three, four, and five years old. Parents were never there for them then, or didn't know how to talk to children.** Then problems come out when these kids are teenagers, and parents get all frustrated. But it's almost too late to deal with it then.

RH: It sounds like you're talking about massive doses of parent re-education.

RC: Yes. **This might sound funny coming from a parachurch organization like ours that focuses on the teenager. And I deeply believe in my work, but in terms of training your kids, the most important time is from ages 0-10. We don't emphasize that fact in the church.** When we talk about youth work, we talk about junior high and high school. I believe in that, but it's a different kind of youth work. What you're doing then, as a youth worker, is building on whatever's been put in that kid's life by that time.

RH: So, if you're the pastor or the chairman of the deacons — or whatever — at the local church, and you have the opportunity to express your influence with this thing called youth ministry, what do you specifically do for the kids 0-10 years of age?

RC: A minute ago I said that time spent with your teenagers is different than time spent when they're younger. They *want* to spend time with the parent as a youngster. They want to be with you. They want to talk with you. They want to play ball with you, tickle you. Those things are very, very important. **As a pastor, the first thing I'd do is to set up courses to help young parents. When they have a baby — bang! — they're in a course. They're going to have the most important years with their kids then,** so here's what to do. I'd really emphasize that. I'd emphasize a lot of church programming that allows younger couples with younger kids to be together in various settings.

RH: Mentoring and nurturing.

RC: Exactly. Now when kids become teenagers, they typically don't want to be with their parents. They don't want to talk with their parents. That's okay. But my experience is that kids still want their parents there. They just don't have the same kind of relationship with you as they did when they were young. You walk in the door as the parent of a youngster and they want to be seen with you. They want to hang on you. But when they hit that teenage moment, they don't want to be seen with you. But it's very important that you are around, that you show up to games and concerts and school stuff. Don't make a big deal out of it. But don't miss those times, because they'll know that you're not there.

Ginny Olson

Be available during adolescent years. Adolescents are developing an independence from their parents. But they still

desperately need to know that parents are there. So often the parent will choose to go to work when the child hits junior high, and that is the time that kids need to know more than ever that their parents are available. "I come home from school," they say, "and I want to tell you stories of how the day went." Instead, they have to wait until 6:00 p.m. Then there's dinner. Then there's homework. And the stories never get told. Parents don't realize that they just need to be hanging out with the kid. The kid is often ready to talk when they're there. That's hard. That takes a lot of time.

RH: How about the parents who both have to work? How do you still try to show your availability?

GO: I think of one parent who moved a rocking chair into the kitchen, and so when the parent was cooking dinner, there was a place where the kid could come in and sit. That parent was saying, through certain signs, "I am here and ready to listen, even though I'm busy. You are a priority, and I want to turn my attention to you."

Marlene LeFever

Major in the majors. Looking at what things are happening in the life of your kid, ask yourself, "Is this major, in terms of where my child is going?" For example, if a teen decides to get a tattoo on their forehead that's a Satanic symbol, that might be a major. But getting a fourth pierce in their ear or nose for a ring, is that major? **We need to look both at what things this generation is doing in order to separate themselves from the generation before it and at those things that are dangerous. Things that are not dangerous, let's not go to the wall for.**

RH: You're saying that subcultures are so different, let's be careful how we choose our battles?

ML: Every culture is different — and if it's not — something is wrong with the culture. Teens have got to say something about who they are. They do it in strange ways, sometimes based on

our definitions of strange. But when you look back on certain things that other generations did, they're every bit as strange. We forget that.

David Olshine

I'd say, "**Get a life! Grow up!** You have intentionally planned to have a child, or maybe you didn't. But you're stuck now. So, grow up. **Stop whining about not making enough money or not having enough time. Get back to what you really need to be doing with your kids. Better do it now, or you'll regret it.**"

I think that Steven Covey, in his *Seven Habits of Highly Effective People*, simply calls it "begin with the end in mind." Covey talks about imagining a funeral. You're going to this funeral and you walk up to the casket and it's you! You look in and there's your body. People are standing up to talk about you. **I think that all parents need to ask the one obvious, serious question: "What will my kids say about me? Honestly, what would they say about me even behind closed doors that they might not say about me in public?"** Covey says, if that one question is asked, then answered by a parent, they'll work backwards to the goal. If I want my kids to say, "My dad was always at every one of my cheerleading games. He was always at every one of my basketball games," you don't start working at that when you're 69 years old. You start early. So I say to all parents, "Get to it! Get to the task!"

Dennis McCluen

First, make a plan. What are they committed to, as parents? What are their priorities? They have to be proactive in their parenting, not reactive. What do they want for their children? What are their hopes, desires and goals as Christian parents? **I see too many problems surfacing — not because parents are not smart, not because they don't care, not because they don't love**

> I see too many problems surfacing because parents don't have a plan.

their kids — but because they don't have a plan. So have a plan, be proactive, and, lastly, don't believe that you're not needed. It's a cultural lie that every kid loves to tell their parents. **Every study shows that parents are still the most significant influence on their kids.**

Rick Dunn

Number one is **"Learn to grieve and to grow."** The key to being an effective parent is being able to **work through your disappointments and hurts when kids don't do what you want them to do.** And I'm not talking about the kid who radically rebels. **Eventually kids disappoint you.**

And, keep growing yourself. Because the number one model that kids need is the model of a parent who is growing in their relationship with the Lord. **They don't need a perfect parent; they need a growing parent!** And, if you are grieving and growing, then your kids are learning that also, so they are much more equipped for their own life. And **your home becomes a place where it is safe for people to struggle and grow.** You don't have the dysfunctional problems which come from ignoring or pretending or controlling.

Harold Ivan Smith

I'm very concerned about over-activities-oriented churches. Parents need to take a strong look here. **There is a sense in which we expect the youth minister to be psuedo-parent, to do what we used to call *in loco parentis*.** We have now turned that over to the youth minister. He's the "specialist," and he'll develop all this stuff. What bothers me is people who are at the church every night of the week. That in itself can produce enormous amounts of stress. Suddenly there is very little time for families to be together because there's something at the church all the time. One question parents have to decide is how much to participate in the church's menu of activities. Particularly if a long distance is involved, driving time becomes a factor as well.

RH: I thought you were going to take off on the youth pastor as specialist — *in loco parentis* — not just the time factor, but who's running the show. Does that factor out the parent's responsibility for being more directly (as opposed to indirectly) involved?

HS: That's exactly right, and one of the issues is how much a parent knows about the youth program. When churches traditionally relied on a kind of network of parents, the youth program was basically parents running it. Now, by hiring a professional, parents are only peripherally involved. In some places there's the attitude "that's what we pay you to do." **There's a sense in which the youth ministry can become a baby-sitter.** Or consider the immaturity of a sizable number of people who are leaders within youth ministry. That's very scary to me: that we have turned over a generation of teens to "other teens," who are not chronological teens, but there's this incredible desire to bond with them. I watched this the other day. I wanted to say to this man, "You are fifty years old; you are not a teen. Quit trying to act like one."

There's such an idolization of youth. Many parents have assumed, "Well, you know, the church must have thought through this hiring of a youth pastor. Obviously this professional person must know what they're doing. They can run a good program." But there is a difference between running a good program and running a ministry with youth. Increasingly we have settled for an activities model of youth ministry, which bothers me, because **I'm wondering what the next generation of church leaders is going to be like. That's a scary thing.**

Mark Cannister

My message to parents is that **parents need to work hard at communicating with their teenagers.** They really need to focus on their teenagers when they communicate. So when the teenage daughter comes home after school and is trying to communicate with Mom, Mom needs to put the dishes down and really focus on what her teenager is saying, not continue to do the dishes. If she's watching TV, turn the TV off and give full attention to the teenager. If Dad's outside changing oil in the car and there's an opportunity for some communication, put down the tools and talk. **Give undivided attention like we've never done before.**

The other thing that goes along with that is accepting and being open to what it is that the teenagers are actually communicating. Let them know that, as a parent, you're glad that they're communicating with you. There's a sense of acceptance; there's a sense of wanting to know; there's a sense of real curiosity on the part of the parents. I think **the church would do well to teach parents some communication skills,** teach parents the art of asking questions and using different levels of probing. Instruct how to create a conversation and how to get beyond the "yes-no" kinds of questions.

Len Kageler

Two things. **First, a parent must learn to acknowledge their teen's feelings.** For example a kid will say, "I can't get my homework done." And a typical parent will say, "If you just studied harder" or "If you didn't watch as much TV . . ." That could be appropriate advice, but that's not what kids need to hear as the first line of strategy. The first thing the parent should say is, "You must be really frustrated," or, "That's disappointing, isn't it?" **Kids are crying out to be heard. And in being heard they ascribe values.** They're saying: "If you don't listen to me, you don't value me." And many parents go right to the advice mode first. That's not what kids need. They first need parents who have learned how to acknowledge the feelings of their kids.

> Kids are crying out to be heard.

That concept really transformed our family when we got ahold of it. For example, one of our kids would come home, and she had lost something at school and she was just fuming. A typical parental response is to get angry back, to escalate things. But we learned pretty early on in her adolescence that this is how she expresses stress. So we've learned how to say, "This must be really disturbing to you," or, "That's so disappointing." And it's just defused so much tension.

Another piece of advice: All parents know that their kids are not the same, but **parents don't generally have a good handle on birth-order characteristics.** Your first-borns are usually one way, and your second-borns are usually the ones that are much more peer-oriented, materialistic-oriented, much less amenable to rules and structure. And a parent who thinks that they're experts with the first one, when the second comes, they're blindsided because the second and first are so different. There are a lot of resources out there on the birth order.

Helen Musick

One of Jay Kesler's great pieces of advice is to understand that teenagers don't want to be put in a cage. But they do want to be put on a leash. There's security in boundaries and in knowing that there's someone who loves them enough to say, "This is how far you can go and no farther." I work with sixteen juvenile centers, teenage girls who are results of no boundaries, of no leash. And 99% of their parents are so self-absorbed that they don't have the emotional or social ability, probably, to even give their kids any structure.

One of Jay Kesler's great pieces of advice is to understand that teenagers don't want to be put in a cage. But they do want to be put on a leash.

RH: Helen, what would be some examples, from working with those girls, that help you realize that, yes, teens want a leash? Some boundaries?

HM: When they're in prison they're scared to leave because they know that, on the outside, they don't have any security, no structure saying, "You can or cannot do this." **I've heard a girl, more than once — in fact several girls — say, "I feel loved here in this juvenile center. I feel *safe* here." And safety for them is love. Safety is security.**

What's one piece of advice you wish to give to every parent?"

Dan Bautista

Not only as a parent of two teenagers, but after working with parents and youth — both in English and in Spanish — I think it is good to maintain open communication. There are different kinds of communication. Sometimes you talk, but you also need to be there to listen. **We have a lot of older Hispanics around, and once a month we try to get a grandpa or someone to tell us the history of the revolution or history of the valley, what happened when Texas was becoming a part of the great Union of the United States.** There are times when you just listen. Listen and learn. You must have an open line of communication.

Also try to maintain trust on both ends. You must be trustworthy as a parent. Teens must trust you, and you must be able to trust them. That's one of the problems a lot of the churches are having. They don't trust teenagers and what they can do.

RH: If parents were to hear you, then say, "Yes, we want that; where do we start?" what would you tell them?

DB: For example, pretend there is a home of an elderly person, and it needs a new roof (this actually happened in our neighborhood) and one of the youth groups said, "We can help them. We can do it." But the church said, "No, you're teenagers, you can't do it." Say that the project began anyway. And once the project got started, church leaders wanted to have one of the adults control the money — instead of letting the kids control the money — to do the shopping for materials that were needed. Next, the adults didn't believe that the kids could learn about safety in order to climb on the roof to do the actual work. So they hired a contractor to come and help them out. **The whole project became a really important part of the youth ministry: challenges regarding the management of money, telling the truth, and adults being able to say, "Yes, you can do it." That brings total trust.** Hispanics tend to learn more from watching people do things. Although second generation Hispanics tend to be more inclined to read instructions, then do it, first generation Hispanics would rather watch you do it, and then they can do it. So a cooperative effort is necessary. Teens often only need some guidance.

Wayne Rice

Protect the relationship that you have with your kids. Keep those communication lines open. The primary way to do that is while children are younger, so that the transition into adolescence isn't so abrupt. If you never talk with your young kids, you never do things with your kids, you never spend time with your kids, it's a little difficult to start that when they're fifteen. But it's all a matter of a relationship.

Children respond to power and authority, but adults don't. Since teenagers are young adults, when parents try to lead with just their power and authority, it's no wonder that teenagers rebel. Parents themselves would rebel if their own parents were still treating them like teens. **But if someone is treating you with dignity and respect, someone's taking your ideas seriously, and there's a little bit of a mutual sharing of the power that's going on — which of course is something that all parents should do — then there's a relationship exhibiting obedience and grace.** As Steve Glenn puts it, "If you will take teenagers seriously and treat them with dignity and respect, they will give you great power and authority over them." But if you try to take it, it ain't going to happen. But it all comes from the kind of relationship that you have with your kids. So you begin to let out the rope and change the nature of the relationship.

People sometimes say, "When your kids become teenagers, they're going to seek their own identity, and you just have to let go," but my feeling is that it's not so much a matter of letting go. Rather it's changing the relationship that you already have established.

Thom Schultz

Encourage your kids to talk. Relationships, honor, trust, and especially faith grow out of dialogue. They don't grow out of listening to somebody lecture. Dialogue is so important, and it's one of the features desperately missing in contemporary homes.

RH: So, how do you encourage kids to talk?

TS: We learn how, as parents, to ask good questions. We ask questions that aren't loaded. We ask questions that we don't already know the answers to. We ask questions that don't contain *the* answer that we are looking for, but are good, open-ended questions.

Another bit of advice is to make story-telling a family sport. Then we become a family of stories. Each time the family gathers, whether it's in the evening or the morning, build a tradition of sharing stories. It works

Make storytelling a family sport.

that way in our family. When we get together, the first thing anyone says is, "Tell me your stories from the day." We become better and better at storytelling. **It's through the activity of talking and sharing our lives — through story — that we get to know one another. We deepen our relationships. We deepen honor and trust and faith.**

RH: Tell me how you think storytelling specifically helps faith development?

TS: Faith development has been seen by parents and church leaders as a spectator sport. You listen to the sermon. You listen to the Sunday school teacher. You listen to the youth leader. But that's *not* the way faith develops. **We have to enter in and be a part of faith formation. We don't simply sit and passively listen. As we become engaged, our faith grows.** We vocalize what faith means to us — things like how our faith is growing, what we think about that, how we see God working, and what we think about God.

RH: And it would seem with today's movement towards a more visual learning society, that your advice would match up with many contemporaries in our society who stress word pictures, not just abstract letters. For better or for worse, that really parallels the oral tradition of the Old Testament.

Mike Yaconelli

First of all, let's take the gospel seriously. Let's tell the truth. Let's quit lying. Life is hard and complicated; it's messy;

> Let's tell the truth. Let's quit lying. Life is hard and complicated; it's messy; it's difficult; it's not simple.

it's difficult; it's not simple. Let's quit describing the gospel in ways that are impossible to live — and nobody is living them. When we say to kids, "You need to give 100% of your life to Jesus," nobody does that. It's never done. It's never been done. It never will be done. There is no such thing as 100%. I may give 70% this morning when I wake up and be down to 20% by tonight. Let's talk about reality. Let's tell the truth. Let's be real in church, because if you are real then people are truly safe. If I know that everyone else there is telling the truth and being real, then I have someplace I can be safe. Kids are not safe in church, and they need to be. Neither are adults for that matter. So we need to create the proper atmosphere.

RH: Truth telling.

MY: Yes. It's real simple. We just believe in the truth and then we tell them. Secondly, what is a parent's job? **A parent's job is not to create perfect kids. A parent's job is to, first of all, help kids find what their calling is. When you look at the Old Testament, they continually named their kids with their dreams for their child.** So, in the Old Testament, your name was kind of a prophetic dream. Samuel was "heard of God." So, every time Hannah called Samuel, she was saying, "heard of God," "heard of God," "heard of God." Working that into his very identity. **Our role as parents is to help kids discover: What are your gifts? Where have you been called? What makes you so valuable and necessary?** The second thing we need to do is **we need to affirm our kids. People are starved for affirmation. We're so beat up. And church is one of the primary places where we get beat up. We continue saying to parents, "You're not doing a good enough job. If you were living the way Jesus wanted you to, your kids would turn out great." Really?** Well then, explain to me why Esau and Jacob — when they came out of the womb — why Jacob was grabbing Esau's foot trying to pull him back in? Where did that come from? Those parents didn't even have a chance to parent yet.

"What's one piece of advice you wish to give to every parent?"

Parenting is overrated. I think that, obviously, we love our kids. We can damage them or we can help them by what we do. **But our job is to affirm these kids and tell them how neat they are, how much we love them. Tell them how cool they are — not just with our words, but with how we look at them and how we treat them and how important we show they are.** All this stuff that we've heard like saying "no" and all that — that's all good and true and right — but, at the same time, the parents that I'm running into over and over again have stopped saying anything nice to kids. Once they get hormones, that's the end of it. From that moment on it's "Where were you? What were you doing? Who's car was that? Where did you get those clothes? Take the makeup off. Why are you doing this?" And all of a sudden we wake up one day and our kids are leaving. The biggest shock to me was when I sent my first kid to college. I just broke into tears realizing, I'm done! Where did it go?

Parenting is overrated.

Celebrating our kids, that's the other thing. We're too serious. My favorite story is about the parents who had a seventeen year old who was into heavy metal, leather, earrings. They were just not getting along. Both parents worked, and it was just dividing them because every time they came home, he was listening to heavy metal music. It was driving them crazy. And a counselor came to them and said, "Ok, here's what I want you to do. When you come home tonight, go down to his bedroom and say, 'Johnny, get out of the bedroom, turn that music off, get up to the kitchen, sit down and shut up. We want to have a talk.' And when he gets up there he'll have an attitude, and it'll take him ten minutes, and he'll be all ticked off, and he'll slump in his chair." Then the counselor added, "You look at this kid and go, 'All right, John, your mom and I are counting to 100, now go and hide.'" And can you imagine, that next day, the kid saying, "I played hide and seek with my parents until 3:00 in the morning"? You know, I've told this story a million times. People have done it, and they've responded, "This was such a breakthrough."

Parents are so uptight. Kidnap your kids from high school. The schools tell us we can't do that. Well, they're wrong! I can

Kidnap your kids from high school. **take my kids from school anytime I want to, to spend time with them for the day** — an unexcused absence — I don't have to lie — and I say to my kid, "I just want to spend the day with you. We're not going to have a big heavy talk. We're going to go water skiing. We're going to take a hike. We're just going to be together because, man, I love you. I don't have many days like this, and I want them now. I just want you to know how much I love you and care about you." **What does it take to write your kid a note and sneak it in their lunch and say, "You are the neatest kid"?** That kind of stuff, that's what's needed.

Haman Cross

Parents — before they become parents — need to be exposed to good role models with good principles. They need to listen and interact with parents and grandparents who have had struggles and successes, so they get a sense of life. **They need to know where they're going before they get there. Before they become parents — and before their kids become teenagers — they could never listen to too many war stories — or examples of earlier parents who excelled and were successful.** In other words, let's say that a parent has a certain philosophy about punishment or how to help a kid select a career. There are enough seasoned parents around who — twenty or thirty years down the road — will show the younger parent what they're going to look like if they follow that particular viewpoint. That connection with the older generation is necessary.

RH: Any suggestions on how that is done? I hear you saying there's a need for intergenerational education.

HC: It can be started at a local church level. **One strategy that has become extremely popular for us has been a church retreat. In the last five or six years the highlight of that retreat was to have a council meeting of our elders. Four or five of our men in their seventies lead a panel discussion.** Up to 250 young men will simply ask them questions. Questions about everything. That's the most popular session on the retreat. **These old, wise, spiritual men are able to scratch where the younger guys itch.** Many of them bond to these older men because their grandfathers are not around.

I just got back from Uganda and it's the same challenge there. Because now that TV is part of their culture, all the kids want to be Americans. They had their elders describe ancient African traditions at this national youth conference. Now these younger kids know the traditions, but did not know the meanings for them or why they even did them. So, again, at this conference with several thousand teens, a panel of elders was the most popular section. These young adults had hundreds of questions for the older men. It was a forum for them to talk. There was some bonding that took place and there were some relationships that were established. Now the younger people know who the ancient ones are in their village or city or church. And I think that the church and families should follow that example.

I'm trying to establish a tradition in my family that my children ask my parents questions — like what it was like when they were raising me or what the problems and challenges were.

RH: Like it's said, there is a point when people realize that the more things change, the more they haven't. That concept connects each generation.

HC: Absolutely, and **there are important principles that cross all generational lines.** We have to go back and remove the ancient boundaries. We have to go back and repair things. For example, my son was recently talking with my dad about how he started his ministry. Then my son saw us start the church here where I pastor. So he has this legacy in his blood. Someone starting a church or a business. Now he asks me questions like, "How did you do it?" and, "What were the challenges?" It's just natural. Somehow we have to reconnect.

Chapter 4
"Musts" of Christian Parenting

If it came down to one nonnegotiable quality or task of Christian parenting, what would that be, for you?

Thom Schultz

My encouragement to parents is to start with ourselves. If *our* lives aren't first in order, and we aren't growing on this journey — deepening *our* relationship with God and with one another in the family — it's hopeless to think that something else is going to work with our kids. Whenever we have an employee problem here, we can often trace the cause back to that person's background. It often relates right back to their family environment. If we've got somebody here, for example, who's a chronic rescuer — a leader who is inappropriately "rescuing" everyone at every turn — when we look at their family life and how their parents interacted with them, what we often find is that their parents were also rescuers in an unhealthy way. **So our life and faith as parents needs to grow naturally, in unscripted ways.**

Then we need to invite our kids into our lives and show them our consistency in different settings. As I was talking with one of our people here yesterday, he was relating a story about when he was a kid. His dad always seemed to act a certain way, fairly mature and responsible. That's how he knew his dad. **But one day his dad invited him to come along with him and his buddies after work. He saw a whole different — and unseemly — side of his dad that he had never seen before. He heard his dad use words he had never heard before and act in a way he had never seen. It did a lot of damage.** Our kids need to see the consistency of who we are in different settings, not just when we're at home with them in front of the fireplace. **Our kids also need to watch us engage in problem-solving, in handling adversity, and how we show compassion to one another.** These are natural life examples that speak volumes without us even having to say one word.

Ron Habermas: So, it's real life stuff, this thing called consistent modeling. Otherwise you fall into the trap of the basic Pharisaical problems found in the New Testament.

TS: Modeling by going out of our way to invite our kids into the different corners of our lives. Take them to work with us. Take them on trips with us. Take them on social visits we have with our peers. Let them see how we act out our lives and, hopefully, display a Christian lifestyle in all sorts of settings.

Dennis McCluen

Someone said that the family has got to be the place where three basic needs of children are communicated: Kids are loved, they're valuable, and they are never alone. If those driving needs are not met in the family, then they are going to be met somewhere else in society. So the nonnegotiable, as parents, is "How am I going to tell my kids that they are loved, they're valuable, and they're never alone?" "Never alone" means that no one will ever give up on them.

The church is there to meet those same needs, but in a supportive role, not a primary role. Also, a nonnegotiable for Christian parents is to share their faith with their kids. And we are to teach life skills to them.

Rick Dunn

God called me, as a parent. I am not commanded to make my kids turn out okay! My responsibility is to Him. I am to be a godly person and parent, not to make my kids godly. The reason I say that is because if my goal is to make them turn out a certain way, then I am always parenting them, and Christ is there just to get things straightened out. However, if I am parenting out of obedience to the Lord and I am growing, then **I view parenting as a process whereby my child is being regularly delivered into God's hands, as His child.**

I did a parenting seminar one time and this lady came up to me and said "I want to thank you for your presentation. I almost didn't come because I didn't want to hear one more thing I'm doing wrong." That was what she thought a Christian parenting seminar would be: telling her what she should be doing as a parent. Instead, we talked about where we go from where we are. Like, if you have a kid who is struggling and you say: "I've got a fifteen year old who is starting to lie to me. Christian kids don't lie; I have to nip this thing in the bud" versus "I've got a fifteen year old who is lying to me; something is going on here. God help me learn to provide the best nurture, love, discipline, direction, and correction. Not only change their behavior, but their heart as well." Because when kids get to be teenagers they can't be controlled like kids. I think this is a huge issue. And it causes all sorts of parental guilt.

Dan Bautista

One of the nonnegotiables is trust. Once teens lose trust in you — and you in them — then it's all over. A parent needs to be able to trust their young people. Now, if you can't do that, then that's what you need to work at first. A lot of problems with the youth today are either because they don't trust their parents or their parents don't trust them. **When you talk about church activities or youth trips — even just teaching the Bible — teens need someone they can trust and someone who can trust them as well.**

> Once teens lose trust in you — and you in them — it's all over.

Wayne Rice

The nonnegotiable feature at the top of the list would be prayer. My wife and I covenanted many years ago to pray for our kids every day. But besides praying daily for your kids — which affects a lot of what you do as a parent — you should be modeling. You can't preach at your kids. When they become teenagers, it's too late to preach at them, as parents. My friend, Stan Beard, said once, "When my kids were little I used to talk to them a lot about God. But when they became teenagers, I started talking to God a lot about my kids." I think that is true.

You pray and then you just live. **You live the kind of life in front of your kids that you're trying to get out of your kids. Some parents are threatened by that because they think it means you have to be perfect. But that's not true at all.** In fact, just this week we had a serious breakdown in communication with our son. We both just went huffing and puffing to our respective bedrooms. The next day, I sat down with Corey and said, "I really need your forgiveness; I don't think I was hearing you; I wasn't listening very well." And he put his arms around me. As parents, sometimes we need to model, "Hey, I blew it, and I need to make that right with you." **At his age, that does tons more than giving him a lecture on learning to show respect to other people. You model it. That's what our Lord says.** It's *not so much saying* just the right things, *but doing* the right things.

Les Parrott

It's going to sound flippant, but the bedrock is love. Out of that come all kinds of good things. Love that's expressed through God's grace in their own lives. Through that come other qualities like forgiveness and empathy.

Mark Senter

I agree, it's unconditional love. But I would add a twist. Let's put it this way: **I think that we need to allow kids to go from *eros*,** to *phileo,* to *agape.* **I think there is a normal progression that children go through.** To first have a feeling-oriented phase, then to learn to become a friend, finally to grow into an unconditional lover. We need to honor all three of those in our families, rather than condemning *eros* as only bad, lustful expressions. In the best sense, *eros* is also that gutsy, emotional quality. It's passionate and positive. **We need to celebrate all three kinds of love in a natural, developmental way.**

Mark Cannister

The big, nonnegotiable would be creating logical consequences rather than punishment. Wayne Rice talks a lot about this in his *Understanding Your Teenager* seminar, and I think that he's really right. When we get into the punishment mode, we typically move out of the educational mode. And it's important to start at an early age. If a teenager comes home too late for dinner, they miss dinner. That logically makes sense to them and to their parents. If they're not driving in a sane manner, then they're not going to be driving. **All of those things need to be negotiated up front so that when the infraction occurs, you avoid the blow-up scene.** It's a much more logical, rational consequence of their behavior than some irrational punishment that's laid down on them.

Harold Ivan Smith

I would call it "expressed love." **Expressed love means devising ways to make sure that the teenager finds and knows that she is loved.** I had a father who never told me that he loved me. I assumed that, but he never told me until he was facing heart surgery. I was 36 years old. I really wish I had heard that a lot earlier, during my teen years. One Scripture passage that fascinates me is when Jesus, as He comes up out of the Jordan after His baptism, hears these words, "This is my beloved Son in whom I am well pleased." And I look at that and go, "Well, Jesus hadn't done anything at that point." That was the start of His ministry. That phrase would have made more sense, in one way, at the cross, or at the Last Supper, or somewhere like that. But I think those words echoed through Jesus' mind all those years of ministry. We, as parents, need to create ways to creatively express love — other than just buying kids things — by giving them quality time when we're with them. Then that echoes through their minds: "My parents love me. My parents expressed their love for me."

I see an awful lot of kids who don't hear that; they don't see spontaneous affections. That is so important. I know some teens don't want to be hugged, but nevertheless, it's still that reaching out to the son, reaching out to the daughter: "You are special to me. You're very important to me." I know one father who raised incredible kids. Often he was on the road, and he would come in very late. But he would still go into their bedrooms and kneel and pray. **I had one of his sons, as a seminary student, and he would tell me what it was like to be half asleep and wake up and hear his dad praying for him.** The power of that experience — of knowing that his dad was praying for him — was an important factor for him.

The most creative way my dad expressed his love for me (and I've never forgotten it because I think about it every fall) was this: We had to do this leaf collection when I was in the seventh grade. We had to identify all these different leaves. So my dad went out and took a piece of cardboard and walked through I don't know how many acres of woods until he found sixteen types of leaves. Then when it was all labeled he brought it back to me. I had already found leaves from the maple and the oak trees, simple ones like that. But his collection was much more sophisticated. I remember that he was tired, but he tramped off and did that. It was his way of expressing his love for me, in what was little more than a science project. But it was so much more, and I value that now, many years later. That is a very important memory to me.

Len Kageler

First, **have an incarnational approach to parenting.** We are modeling and incarnating Christ in our families, to our spouses, and to our children. We, as youth workers, also want to incarnate Christ to people in our church groups. So parents need to incarnate a Christlikeness in the home. That, of course, means the fruit of the Spirit. That means grace and mercy and listening and sensitivity. All the things that Jesus shared.

I've seen some pretty unhappy settings where the father views himself as the master, the authority. Everybody has to toe the line, or they're in deep trouble. Christ had authority, but it was generally a relational-based authority or an authority based on perceived competence, as opposed to a positional-based authority.

Another nonnegotiable should be — and this should come easy for most Baby Boomers — to be real with their kids. To acknowledge their own vulnerability, their own frustration, and to seek the prayer of their own children as well as their help. **The family becomes a Christian support group, as opposed to the parents always being in the authoritative teaching mode.** That mode does not work so well anymore. That's a point I make in my book, *Teen Shaping*, by Revell. As a parent and as a kid, we both come to the Scripture on the same level — in terms of how the Holy Spirit can speak to my kid as clearly as He can speak to me. That helps to transform how we see the family and our parent's role in it.

Leith Anderson

Realizing that God is actually the real parent of their teens. I think that adults perceive that *they* are the parents and that they have the responsibilities of God, rather than perceiving that *God is the parent,* and they are the agents of God in the parenting role. That difference of perspective has enormous theological and practical ramifications to it.

God is the ultimate parent. There's great comfort — when your children don't turn out as you chose for them — to recognize that God had other children in Scripture that didn't turn out as He chose.

RH: So it would be comparable to the idea of stewardship. That I, as a parent, do not own these particular teens, but I am the one who takes care of them.

LA: Yeah, that we are the agents of God in our children's lives for a certain period of time, and that our role differs from chapter to chapter. **God is the ongoing and ultimate parent. There's great comfort — when your children don't turn out as you chose for them — to recognize that God had other children in Scripture who didn't turn out as He chose for them, as well.**

David Olshine

Probably there are two issues for me. One would be the need for the natural infusion of the truth of God — God's Word — into a family. And the second would flow out of that — actually it may be more functional — the whole idea of communication: honest communication, open communication. **When I meet parents of teenagers they're basically saying, "I don't really know how to talk to my kids."**

RH: Could you explain that first issue?

DO: If I'm going to call myself a Christian, I have to ask myself a serious question: "Does my life make any difference in the world? Do we, as a family, look any different than a pagan family?" **Judeo-Christian truth (from Deuteronomy 6) means that the truth of God is infused naturally — when you rise up, when you go to bed, when you're walking, when you're talking, when you're laying down. It's natural. It's not forced. It's not lecture.** But oftentimes, it's only talked about. Yet, even if you're watching a TV show, you're able to give your kids good values, asking them, "How could this show help our family to be more godly?" I think that at the heart of that education is prayer and teaching our kids how to pray and praying with them. I've known many families who have stopped doing that when their kids get a little bit older.

RH: Could you say more about teaching kids to pray? And are there any other particular skills which help that become natural?

DO: You must realize that you've got only a few years left to teach skills to your kids in particular areas of life and giftedness. One of those areas is autonomy. I realize that my daughter, Rachel, has a natural bent towards athletics and cheerleading. I can also see areas where she's not really strong, like finances. So this year we're going to work with her on that. We're going to get her a checkbook and work with her on these weak skills. **I think that these are "natural things" that any parent should be doing: finding where kids are strong, applauding it, encouraging them to do it. And, at the same time, finding areas where they need to grow and charting out a plan.** So the next two years we're going to work with her on setting a budget, giving Rachel some money, starting a checkbook, and letting her learn to play with it.

Ken Davis

Demonstrations that my love for my kids is unconditional. I can't think of anything else that would lead kids to want to experience Christ, that would lead kids to compassion for other people, and that would lead them to a solid understanding about who they are — a good, solid psyche about their own worth — than that. **And grace is the foundation of everything that I believe is worth living for. Grace has to be demonstrated.**

Mike Yaconelli

Tell the truth. Be real. Trust the truth. I'm divorced. I have five children. My kids have been through an awful divorce. I could easily go, "Well, I screwed up. It's over. What's the point? I've broken the commitment. Obviously, my kids are all screwed up. I have no right to say anything to them." But I just have to live the gospel. I live the forgiveness, the grace, the confession of sin, the failure, the humiliation. And I trust — in the middle of all that — that they will see the truth. I have to trust in that plan.

Tell the truth.
Be real.
Trust the truth.

Haman Cross

There needs to be a real sense of vision before you start. What is it that you want to accomplish? There needs to be a commitment to partnership. A real appreciation for your mate's differences. Respect their thoughts. And it really requires dignity. There are values that I want in my daughters that are in my wife.

> There needs to be a real sense of vision before you start.

Our kids need both of us. **Vision is partnership.** That takes talking and negotiating. I think that it really helps kids, in the long run, when the couple consists of two different personalities. My wife is completely different than me — in a whole lot of ways — and that is so healthy, because my kids can see two opposite individuals working together. My son has all the confidence in the world — a confidence that says, "Look, I want to marry somebody different." So I think that a couple doesn't need to water down their differences.

RH: Then, we must celebrate differences.

HC: That is the best training in life, because when your kids get out in the world, everybody is different. And **we've gone though generations of Christians who lived by themselves and who were not involved in the world. Part of our cross-cultural problem is not fulfilling the role of the church. Traditionally, we were never encouraged to celebrate our diversity.**

Roger Cross

The nonnegotiable lesson is that more is caught than taught, that the way you *are* speaks louder than what you *say*. So a nonnegotiable for me is that Christian parents be vulnerable about their faith. Like the struggles that they're going through. So many times kids look at their Christian parents and say, "My Christian parents have it all together. I'll never be like them," or they say, "My dad doesn't have it all together and it's really obvious to me, but he keeps trying to put on that front." **It's respecting** your kids enough that you share with them the honesty of your walk with Christ.

It's respecting your kids enough that you share with them the honesty of your walk with Christ.

Dave Rahn

As a Christian parent I am told to lead in a style that is always characterized as servant leadership. I have a responsibility to the Lord for my activity and leadership. So, my nonnegotiable is, **"Have I done, as a parent, everything that I can do to bring the members of my family to an ever-growing relationship with Christ?"**

Ginny Olson

Parents need to model what they teach. That's such an old piece of advice, but the kids are watching so closely. They say, "You tell me one thing, but do you really live it?"

RH: Any other nonnegotiables?

GO: There're lots of them, like listening, and being able to say when you're wrong. **For a kid to see their parent ask for forgiveness and take steps to resolving conflict is huge for a kid. It's like, "I'm getting an example of how to do this"** and **"Show me how you deal with life when you screw up."**

It's like . . . "Show me how you deal with life when you screw up."

Also, the whole concept of dinnertime conversations and having time to talk and say, "How are you with life?" To tell our stories.

Marlene LeFever

One thing that should never be violated is the trust factor between the parent and the child. If I know that whatever my parent tells me is true and just, and I know that I am expected to be both true and just back to my parents, it sets a high watermark. Sometimes we disappoint each other. But I need to know that, no matter what, my parents will not lie to me; no matter what, I can trust what they say to be true. That plays out in little things. It plays out both when I'm very young and later in life. It plays out in very, very simple things and in more serious matters, like knowing my parents don't cheat on their income tax.

Don't lie to your kids. Let them know, no matter what, they can trust you. They also need to know that you are open to hearing anything they have to say, whether it's good, bad, or indifferent. It doesn't mean you'll accept it without punishment, but you are open to hearing it. Expect them to talk to you. I heard a statistic — which I have no way of proving — that before a child goes to preschool, he's spent more time watching cartoons on television than he will ever spend — *in his entire lifetime* — talking to his father. That pulls you back and says, "Whoa." The communication factor for *every* generation is extremely important.

Jay Kesler

Providing an atmosphere of security and love for the young person to grow up in. That atmosphere also ought to contain a consistent example on the part of the parents. If you have an atmosphere where the young person feels love and feels the security that Mom and Dad are not going to separate — surrounded by this love — and that the parents are living careful, Christian lives in front of the kids, then all the rest of proper parenting is icing on the cake. That's the centerpiece. Parents need to learn to communicate that love, to speak that love, to show that love and that security. They need to affirm kids constantly. The Christian example is not just talking about forgiveness, but forgiving; not just talking about discipleship, but being a disciple of Christ. Incarnational Christian messages are what the home is all about. It is very powerful. I think that wherever it is happening, a kid may rebel for a period of time, but they'll be back. I think you'll see kids, between 15 years to 23, do some experimenting, but by the time they've reached their 26th or 28th birthday, they'll often be back. Many will have discovered, "My mom and dad are on the right track."

Helen Musick

The nonnegotiable would be that parents are the primary caretakers in their child's education. Out of lack of knowledge or lack of responsibility, parents are often not the primary caretakers and educators. **Culture offers other avenues of caretaking and educating that make it hard for parents to compete.** It's very easy, for example, to just let the TV be the educator, looking to it to be the caretaker.

RH: So the cultural competition is stiff out there?

HM: It is *so* stiff. TV, to me, is just one of the biggest roadblocks to parenting. I know it's radical, but we got rid of our TV for a couple of years. We've got it back now, but we did away with it, and it had an incredible impact on our lives. For instance, today, I knew I was going to be talking to you for this interview, and my baby-sitter canceled on me, so I just thought, "Well, I'll put my child in front of the TV." **It's not to say that TV is totally evil, but when kids spend that much time in anything, the influence is great.**

Chapter 5
Marooned Like Gilligan (Helpful Resources)

Pretend that you were marooned on an island, like Gilligan; just you, some teenagers and their parents. If you could select only one resource, of any kind (not counting the Bible), what resource would you choose?

Mark Senter

A frisbee. **Because a frisbee is the international friend-maker.** You would need something to give you a common experience on that island. I think that there is a time on this island where you need to get out in the surf and play with the frisbee. Another time you are using it to splash water on somebody. Sometime you might play ultimate frisbee. There's a lot of things that you could do with it. It doesn't require much skill, but allows everybody to enjoy it together. **What you need is a bonding experience.**

A frisbee

Dave Rahn

Probably a pen and paper. I would try to institute some type of meaningful reflection time together.

Ron Habermas: What would be one or two questions you would assign them?

DR: For example, I had a Bible study with some teens this past week and we were looking at Philippians 2. We came to the verse, "Do everything without complaining and arguing." So I could tell these teens and parents: "Now sneak off by yourself to a little part of the island, and jot down the four things that you would most likely complain or argue about. Then listen to what the Lord says to you about that. And jot down the thoughts that come from Him." That type of reflection.

Wayne Rice

How about two resources? A book and a boat — and not just to get off the island. I bought a boat for our family because my kids like to fish. We've had wonderful times on that boat. And there's nothing like being "trapped" on a boat for three or four hours with one of your kids. Just sitting there waiting for fish to bite, you can talk, and it's a great time.

As a far as a book, one that's been really helpful to my wife and me is H. Steve Glenn's *Raising Self-Reliant Children in a Self-Indulgent World*. It's just a wonderful book on helping children become self-reliant, responsible adults. A lot of that occurs during those adolescent years as kids develop skills and their self-image. The book is about how parents can help that process along.

Harold Ivan Smith

I thought of two. I'm such a believer in children's books. One of them is *Fables* by Arnold Lobel. It contains these wonderful little one-page fables which express the basics of family life. The other book is *Love You Forever* by Robert Munsch. One lady, a single parent, told me that even though her son's a teenager, he still likes to hear *Love You Forever*. That's still in his room. It's a simple children's book, but it's that memorable statement of: "I will love you forever, and I will like you for always." Just an incredible little children's book, but it's another way of creatively expressing love. There is something so powerful about that story, especially if you were marooned on an island where you were spending a lot of time together. **You would need that reminder that you are loved.**

Mark Cannister

I picked a book. One of the best books in this area is Kevin Huggins' book, *Parenting Adolescents*. The thing that I really appreciate about his book is that it's not a formula book like so many others. He provides biblical principles to help parents build their own parenting style, move them and their teens into stronger relationships, then move teenagers toward responsibility and becoming more like Christ. **Huggins enables parents to understand that there are certain things that they can control and there are certain things that they can't control.** That's a real winner as a resource.

Jay Kesler

I would want to have the powerful example of Christian elders who communicated consistent caring and Incarnational living. That would communicate to the kids that they are important, they are valued, they are listened to, they are protected, and they are advised. And I think parents can do this. **This is where the Christian church is probably up against two subcultures. It faces a challenge. First, Asian families without the gospel hold tremendous reverence for older people.** As Asian children watch their own parents revere their parents, it's a three-generation education. Asian kids get the idea about authority and God, without even a biblical reference.

The other community that does this very well is the Jewish community. Jewish kids are raised in an atmosphere where parents communicate to them, "We are the parents." Yet parents value their kids' opinions. They listen to them, and the kids learn

to debate. **These kids are used to presenting their ideas to adults, testing their ideas with their adult counterparts.** It's a subculture that offers a beautiful contribution. And in some ways, as Christians — American Christians who are a lot of times more American than Christian — we have a lot to learn from watching the Asian and Jewish communities.

Helen Musick

I'd pick the dictionary, because the gift of words is limitless. If you were stranded with just those people, the thing that would never grow would be the vocabulary — outside of what those people have — so you'd be very limited. **The gift of language and words and definitions is just something that enables growth.**

RH: Why is that important to you?

HM: Because words allow expression. New words, I think, keep people from being stagnant. It allows growth. **Stagnation is deadly.**

David Olshine

The resource that I want is a Land's End bag that's got a few things in it. **One thing I've got to have is a softball and a frisbee — for the simple reason that I don't think that parents and teens play together. We're stuck out there without much to do. We can learn to play together.**

We can learn to play together.

Thom Schultz

I chose a resource we use at our work camps, our one-week long volunteer service projects with young people every summer. That resource is a stack of 3x5 cards, pencils, and envelopes. Together, they provide a system that we call "Care Cards." I'll explain how it works, and then I'll explain the theory behind it. Each day, each person at the camp (all four hundred people) — whether they're a kid or an adult — is instructed to write out a *Care Card* to every person in their six-person crew. So each day they're writing five other *Care Cards*. Then they drop those cards in envelopes marked for those individuals. At the end of the week each person gets to take their envelope down off the wall and read the cards. **That task of writing requires everybody to look for the good, to look for the giftedness, to look for the things we can be thankful for in the people around us. It tends to change our community.** It changes how we act around one another and what we think of one another. It affects our whole attitude towards group experiences.

RH: So the point is to provide an encouraging word for each individual?

TS: Yes. I might be something like, "I really appreciate how you took time out of everything you had to do today just to listen to me and to find out what I was struggling with." It might be something as simple as, "Your sense of humor really cheers all of us up." Or it might be, "You're so quiet, but you're exactly what our crew needs, because the rest of us are loud and off-the-wall. You bring us back down to earth." We've found that that little spoonful of sugar — you can call it affirmation — is something that we so often overlook in relationships. Particularly when we're trying to form community. It's a powerful, powerful thing. **People, particularly teenagers today, hear so many putdowns. If we can reverse that trend by using a simple tool of affirmation, it's transforming.**

RH: What you are doing not only seems to include changing attitudes teens have about their peers, but in turn, changing behaviors for their future. The adolescent relationship cycle (like the negative example you mentioned of the putdowns) often continues to propagate a behavior that's ungodly when left unchecked. But you get the opposite results with your simple strategy.

TS: Exactly.

Len Kageler

Clearly it would be Kevin Huggins' book, *Parenting Adolescents*. That is by far, in my mind, the most significant thing written to parents that I have ever seen. This book is so biblically-based, so incarnationally-written, it just shines a light on you, as a parent. For example, it points out the foolish motives we have as parents when we speak in certain ways to our kids. I love that book.

Dan Bautista

I sat down with my teenage daughter and one of her cousins to answer this! They thought we must have a CD player and a box of CDs. The two of them agreed. Music is a big issue with adolescents.

> Music is a big issue with adolescents.

Mike Yaconelli

I would want to celebrate, with all my heart, that there are no resources. That I — as a parent — am the resource. That's what is wrong in this culture. All of us are so intimidated. We actually believe that an expert has advice for us. That I couldn't have figured things out for myself. He's the expert and I'm not. **It's time for us to reclaim our legitimacy as genuinely significant people who can make meaningful and significant decisions ourselves. That we can figure out how to be parents all by ourselves. And it's a great moment when you suddenly realize, "Wow, I can do this. I can make decisions."** That, to me, is ultimately the greatest resource.

> I would want to celebrate, with all my heart, that there are no resources. That I – as a parent – am the resource.

Ginny Olson

A toolbox. This would allow them to work together and build something, while providing opportunities for conversation.

Roger Cross

A pencil and paper. I'd give it to the parents and say "I want you to write down everything you can about your growing up years, and I want you to sit down and talk to your kids about it." It would open up dialogue between kids and their parents about how hard it was for their parents. Teens would see that their parents, in some way, struggled with some of the very some things that they struggle with. In a different time, yes, but the issues are the same. That exercise would give a certain vulnerability to the parents, so that the kids could see, "My dad really did have some problems. He wasn't this great, star athlete in high school. He was just a common, everyday Joe. I wonder how he dealt with that?" **For parents to talk about their feelings — how they felt growing up as a kid, the struggle they may have had with their parents — those would be good stories to share.**

Rick Dunn

I'd take two resources: Kevin Huggins' *Parenting Adolescents* and David Veerman's *Parenting Passages*. Both give a good vision for what it means to be a parent in constructive relationships. An even better resource (other than a book) would be a mentoring, godly relationship. Be there to talk with them. Give them feedback. Give them encouragement. Provide a long term perspective.

> Ultimately parenting is not about your kids. It's about you.

Ultimately parenting is not about your kids. It's about you. And if you are dealing with "you" well, then that's going to turn out well in your kids. But if not, you are going to be reacting all the time.

Marlene LeFever

I'd take an anthology of Shakespeare's plays. Written in old English. The old English would throw them. It would make them kind of special. **I think Shakespeare did a phenomenal job on just**

about any experience you could possibly go through: temptation; a fatal flaw in a personality; parents and how they react. That becomes a wonderful handbook of interactive tools for the time we spend on that desert island conversing.

Chapter 6
Insights for Single Parents

If you had the opportunity to advise single parents of teens, what one piece of insight would you want to pass on?

Haman Cross

Number one, they definitely need to avoid being *both* mom and dad. Number two, they don't need to deny the absence of the one who is not there. Finally, they need to review (biblically and socially) the whole concept and value of the extended family. **I have yet to see a positive extended family that does not possess the necessary role models for kids. Also, I think single parents need to realize that they have far more going for them then they have against them.**

Ron Habermas: How does that look in the church? Do you have any examples of actual, intentional relationships that are built? Or is it more spontaneous?

HC: It's got to be both. **We've challenged our church to be "family," to be uncles or big brothers. And that gives me the right**

> I have yet to see a positive, extended family that does not possess the necessary role models for kids.

to love you, challenge you, punish you, and help you. I have tried to set that example, hoping men in the church would pick that up, so that our single women who have sons are not intimidated, wondering if they are going to have to address the male gender issues for their children. We want them to know that we can help and it will not cost them. **We are trying to form what we call "watch care." It involves commitment. Parents really take advantage of this ministry without hesitating to call. All the members in the church consider themselves like family.** Whether it's financial decisions or parenting issues or other things. I think that the pastor of a church can grow that kind of mentality. And it becomes a tradition in their local assembly, and their people become attracted to it.

Len Kageler

In our culture with all of the pressures (like financial and time pressures), **the best thing I can say to a parent is, "It's really hard, isn't it?" Acknowledge their pain.** Single parents are advantaged by networking in a church that can offer a significant youth ministry. I guess that would be one thing. It's really hard to be in a smaller church situation where there's no youth ministry for the kids to participate in.

> The best thing I can say is, "It's really hard, isn't it?" Acknowledge their pain.

It's just so difficult as parents to make a living. When you work full time, you pretty much spend all of your emotional chips at work. There's really not much left for the needs of the teenager. You just admit that fact, and then network, so your kid has significant adults in her life from the youth ministry. Those connections can make up a great amount of help for the kid's needs for a listening ear and for a kind touch.

Mark Cannister

I have to refer to Hillary Clinton's book title: Single parents have got to create a village. One way or another, single parents have got to work hard at creating support systems — creating an extended family, if they don't have an extended family. They obviously know they can't do it all themselves. Their time's usually eaten up by the workday, and they're often barely making enough money to get by, so it's unrealistic to lay even more expectations — or even the same expectations — on single parents (in terms of parenting their teenagers) as we do for a two-parent family.

For a single parent, a few hours invested in developing networks and an extended family structure might pay off even better than spending those same few precious hours directly with their own teenagers.

For a single parent, a few hours invested in developing networks and an extended family structure might pay off even better than spending those same few precious hours directly with their teenagers. Hopefully, over the years, as they create this kind of support system, the teenager will grow up in a community where they could say that they — figuratively-speaking — have many aunts and uncles.

Dave Rahn

Single parents of teens are especially crunched with demands and expectations. **If it's important for parents, in general, to carve out a reflection time, it's even more important for single parents. It's even more difficult, in light of their demands. In their reflection, they need to think about their own personal leadership of their family. They have to expand that question to think about additional resources they have available to help them do their parenting task.** And that's where the church is hugely significant to them: to be able to think of particular church people and particular involvements for their children. Then they need to ask: "Is this a good thing?" or "What do I need?" and "What is my kid's need that I can't provide because of my own limitations?"

111

RH: So what would you advise them if they're unfamiliar with the kinds of churches you're talking about? What would you advise them to look for, or how to augment their personal resources with those helps in the church?

DR: Look for a church that has a very good assimilation-relationship network. Churches that celebrate that as a strength. Churches that know how to connect with people and help people get connected with each other. Those connections are going to be as significant as anything for a single parent. **People connections.**

RH: How do you locate a church like that?

DR: I think that it's trial and error. You've got to visit churches knowing what you're looking for. I wish it was different than that.

RH: And also having a couple of key questions — a couple of descriptors — of what that looks like?

DR: Ask questions like, "If I want to get involved in the church, where do we start?" and "How do we get plugged in?" It's a tough task. You're asking someone to come in and read the culture of a place. I don't think you can do that very quickly.

Roger Cross

I'd say that single parents can be incredibly successful. We have some great models of people who have been raised by single parents. So recognize that you're in a special group, but don't use that as an excuse for not being a good parent, because it can be done. We've got too many positive examples.

Single parents can be incredibly successful. We have some great models.

Secondly, I would say, "You've got to have a support group that you can meet with on a regular basis. Where you can talk about what you're struggling with." That support group is incredibly important.

RH: What would that support group help them with specifically? What kind of support?

RC: How to deal with parenting their kid. All of these parents are often going through the same stuff at the same time, and so one parent is able to say, "My kid's gotten himself into this situation." And another parent says, "We've got the same thing. What are you doing for it?" The parent begins to share. It's a sharing of ideas. **It's the resource for seeing how other people are handling the same situation that they're in. They're not alone.**

Mark Senter

Go back to the faith community. Despite the conservative reaction to the phrase "It takes a village to raise a child," I'm absolutely convinced that that saying is true. So I would say to single parents: cultivate the resources of the village. That means that there are going to be some people that you're going to need to talk to. Sometimes you're going to have to get relief from them because of the tension that you're experiencing. Sometimes you need to share celebrations together — Thanksgiving, Easter, Superbowl Sunday, whatever. There are things that you really need the village to do to help you in that celebrative process.

> Despite the conservative reaction to the phrase "It takes a village to raise a child," I'm absolutely convinced that that saying is true.

Then you're going to need the resources, also, when your kid says, "Nobody else's mom and dad are keeping them from doing this." You can go to the rest of the village and say, "Okay, let me check this out." You now have a sounding board. For most of those people, I would say they need some sort of adult Bible fellowship, Sunday School class, or caring group that is not solely focusing on the struggles that they have as a single parent but that gives them the benefit of community when they need it.

RH: Can you think of anything in particular that the single parent, as opposed to the two-parent home, might need to utilize as a resource from that community?

MS: There's an ebb and flow to parenting. Sometimes you're up as a parent and sometimes you're down. The single parent

doesn't have the benefit of the other person picking them up, and that's where I say it's probably a wise thing to have some sort of way to access supportive people when you're down. Furthermore, it's helpful to bring your celebration to others when you're up, because they need the picking up, too. **The single parent needs to have such good relationships with other people that they can bring joy to other people's lives as well as be picked up by them.**

Leith Anderson

The unspoken — the taboo — in today's culture is to say that single parents are operating at a deficit. The only person on the popular scene that I hear that has the nerve to come right out and say that is Dr. Laura Schlessinger, a secular family counselor and therapist. I don't hear the evangelical saying that. And pastors don't say that because it's too painful to say. **If, as a pastor, I imply anything close to that, I have people who will talk to me afterwards and say, "You just wrote me off. What am I going to do?" But Schlessinger is saying that the best thing that children can have is two parents.** I just did an article for *Single Parent* magazine on this point, and it's a very sensitive topic. I did not address that particular issue, but it's a very sensitive issue to communicate to people that they are operating at a deficit.

RH: What would you actually say to a single parent? What particular advice would you slant toward their needs?

LA: I would say to them, "You've got a very hard job to do, and you need to be creative in finding the resources to do it. Probably more so than a two-parent family." Those resources have to do with relationships and extended family systems. **The ideal for a single parent is to be part of an extended family system where the other pieces of parenting can be contributed by grandparents, aunts and uncles. Now if they're geographically dislocated, that means that they've got to find that support within the church or within other relationships.** I find that (it's mostly single mothers that I would talk to) they are keenly aware of that need and they want to follow that advice. They are deeply fearful that if they do involve someone who is not part of their extended family, they are going to make a worse mistake, and their child is going to be abused by someone that they have given permission to fill a role that isn't being filled. They're frightened.

RH: So how does the church help?

LA: I'll tell you what we used to do. **We used to set up Big Buddy programs. But we got out of the business of doing that because of the dangers in it for us, in terms of whether we can truly accredit somebody. Do we really know these people? Plus the liability issues. So we stopped doing it.** There are other things that we do: We accept intergenerational opportunities, and do some matching up of people, but it is more informal than formal, because of the pitfalls that are involved.

> Well, I hate to say it, but everything that we do, we look at from the ministry side *and* from the litigation side.

RH: And the legal issues?

LA: Well, I hate to say it, but everything that we do, we look at from the ministry side, *and* from the litigation side.

Mike Yaconelli

Number one, you say to single parents, "You can be forgiven" and "You can go on. You're the same person you were when you were married, which means you've also got all kinds of problems." And I say that as a divorced parent.

The thing about divorce is that it's so humiliating because your sin is so public. And it's not just your sin, it's your flaws, your humanness. Everybody sees it. The tendency we have is to try to blame and say, "I did everything I could. I went to counseling. I did this and I did that." Even if that's true, even if you were the one that was divorced — the other person left you — both parties generally contribute to marital decline. Deal with it. Recognize that when you marry somebody new, guess what — a few months into the marriage — you're going to hear the same things you heard in the last one. Because you haven't changed that much. And you won't. Take responsibility for your stuff and then move on. It's not cheap forgiveness.

Believe me, you don't get away with anything when you get a divorce. People that say, "Well, they got this; they got that. They're just going on like nothing happened." They can go on like nothing happened, but something did happen and they're not the same, and they will pay a very high price for what they did, whether the church acted responsibly or not. In other words, the person gets a divorce, and the church may turn the other way and not confront them. They're still not getting away with a thing.

RH: How does that connect with the teenager in the case of the single parent, then?

MY: The parent can't keep apologizing to the kid. Kids are human, and they can manipulate this situation. They tend now to blame everything on the divorce. And at some time or another, you as a parent have to go, "You know what? That's three strikes. That's it. I understand that the divorce was hard.I understand that this was difficult, but now you have to move on. I'm not going to live there anymore. I take responsibility for what I did. I will all my life, but now it's time for you to take responsibility and move on. I'm open. I'm willing to admit whatever you want, but now it's time to move on."

Marlene LeFever

As a church we say, "We give you support. We don't look at why you're single; what you did to get that way. We simply say, 'You've got a child; we love you; we'll support you.' That doesn't mean we're condoning your lifestyle if there was infidelity involved. But it simply means that we're saying your child is not a problem to us. We want to mother and father your child." And how a church succeeds will, I think, demand all the creativity that it can muster. Because there are problems.

I know of one church that did not want any child to attend its Sunday School that did not have their parent attend the

church. Knowing full well that lots of parents would never attend the church, they told any of us who were single — I was single at the time — or who didn't have children, that we were to "adopt" those children who wanted to come for a Sunday morning. I ended up with two girls who were my kids for Sunday morning. The church actually parented them in a very unique way. It was my job to have them sit with me. After we went out for lunch on Sunday, I deposited them back into their real family situation. We talked by phone once a week, and I picked them up the next Sunday morning. This was one way the church played with the whole concept of surrogate parenting.

Some of our church communities are looking for men who will father — who will actually be fathers — to the boys in their area who have no father at home. In one nursery school situation (that I think is absolutely wonderful) the wife is the teacher of the nursery school Sunday school, and the husband assists her. He counts how many kids don't have fathers in the home and then divides the amount of Sunday School time by the number of those children, and that's how much time each child gets to spend on his lap. That's wonderful! What a neat way to live out the parenting.

RH: So, basically, you would say to families in your neighborhood, "Become part of our community; become part of us"?

ML: Generation X is rejecting the concept of traditional church. They're going more into the concept of community. They say: "Tell me your story" and "Be my friend." Through friendship salvation, they ooze into the Kingdom, instead of jump into it. As they do that, churches become smaller, or large churches divided into units. **What we're trying to do is build a family structure that is nonexistent in many homes. I also think it's important to use productive methodologies to help build family. I'm a strong proponent of the jigsaw method and other techniques that allow for classes to stay together in the church, or study groups to stay together.** Using the methods of cooperative learning.

Dan Bautista

Don't be afraid to ask for help. It's hard enough to have a couple raise a teenager. One of my nephews has a single mother. He has spent weeks with me at our camp through the summer. He has said it's hard for her to be by herself. The fact that, sometimes, she doesn't ask for help makes it worse. Also, single moms should resist the temptation to ask their sons to act as their husbands.

RH: Does the church have a particular responsibility in these cases? Is the church doing their job?

DB: Our Hispanic culture dictates that the church has no responsibility over the single parents because, most of the time, their single parents' involvement is their choice. **The church has responsibility to give them spiritual guidance. But as far as raising the kids, it's put back into the extended family. Single parents go to the extended family for help.** They can ask for advice from the deacons, the pastors or the elders, but I don't think that our churches are able and willing to provide such help.

RH: The first line of defense is the extended family?

DB: Right. **Our Hispanic culture is very focused around the extended family. And shame on the family that doesn't help single parents. (Rather than shame on the church.) We have a tradition that, after you are baptized — if something happened to one of your parents — your godparent or your grandparents would take you in.** In a lot of the Catholic — and more and more of the Protestant — single families, this trend is beginning to take on greater popularity. So, these support groups get more involved. But the godparents and grandparents aren't going to do anything unless the single parent makes the move — to ask for their help.

Ginny Olson

That's a hard one. There's a woman I worked with who had a ministry to single parents. She had three kids. We had a lot of conversations about how to handle being a single parent. **The key is that you don't have to be both parents. You just have to be**

one. And that it's important to be with your kids. For example, she would just take out each of her children about once a month. Like: "This is your evening. What do you want to do?" Her son would take her to a driving range to teach her how to hit golf balls. Her daughter would take her to the mall, let her enter her world. **The parent wanted to know "What's fun for you? Let me catch a glimpse of that and join you." The kids knew that they had Mom for a certain amount of time, and that time was just theirs. Not to share with anybody else.**

Jay Kesler

I'd say **"Don't see everything through the prism of single- ness or divorce." Very often, what they say to me is, "Jay, I'm a single parent. And my 17-year-old is giving me trouble." I want them to understand that a 17-year-old can be a handful whether you're a single parent or not!** They tend to telegraph their own guilt, their own sense of pain over this juncture in their marriage or life — whether it be by death or divorce — back into the relationship. **So many things are the same about raising children, either as a single parent or with two parents, that I think that they should be very careful not to always see it through their own guilt.**

The second thing, of course, is **I would encourage every sin- gle parent to take advantage of the extended family of God, the body of Christ, the local church. By a single mother taking her son or daughter to Sunday School, by having them in the youth group, they can find supportive, adult males who will make up the other half for her — better than any other place else in culture. Frankly, one of the great, new roles of the church today is providing this extended family, the body of Christ — surrogate aunts and uncles, surrogate grandpas and grandmas, surrogate brothers and sisters for these families.** So, I would encourage single families to immedi- ately get into a church and ask for help.

I would also encourage the traditional families, especially the women, not to be threatened by these divorced and single women — that their husband can be a responsible male in the life of another

A good looking divorcee in the church can absolutely bring other women to panic.

woman without any sexual overtones. **A good-looking divorcee in the church can absolutely bring some women to panic. But they need to surface that fear, they need to pray about it, talk about it. They need to befriend her. She needs to be surrounded by these women, so that the males can help her.**

Helen Musick

The responsibility is very demanding. **To use that phrase "single parents" a bit differently, I think we also have a generation of another kind of single parent: a typical mother married to a father, in a workaholic situation.**

RH: You're referring to intact families that are single?

HM: Yes, the mother stays home with the kids (so that you technically don't classify them as not having a parent at home) which enables the father to work — and overwork — so that they can have the money that they need. You have a mother who's at home with the kids, from seven in the morning until eight at night, until the dad gets home. It's a different kind of single parent that's not normally talked about.

David Olshine

I'd say: "Know your limitations. Hang in there." **As a child of divorce, I remember my mom struggling with balancing a budget, caring for me, being at work, and having me spend time at home without her.** So I'd say know your limits, because there are limited resources. And I'd say set some pretty clear boundaries, especially if it's a single mom who's having to work a lot. Make your boundaries clear. And third, I'd say encourage youth group attendance for their kids so that they might build some good peer relationships.

RH: What kind of boundaries?

DO: I think that with the latch-key mentality, some kids feel like they have the freedom to do whatever they want while their moms or dads are still at work. So I think that there need to be some clear boundaries. A boundary in our house is no TV — and we're not a single family — but no TV until all the homework's done for the next day. And then another boundary is no more than one hour of TV per day. Those kinds of things.

RH: What about the parent's personal limits? What are some examples of that?

DO: I think that people need to know what they're not good at. I've commonly thought that Adam and Eve in the garden really didn't know their limitations. They didn't really think about the fact that God had given them this large garden to care for. That there are some things He told them not to touch. **I think that a lot of us are interested in touching the things that we shouldn't touch. A single parent needs to realize that the Image of God profoundly comes through both male and female. That's my perspective in a marriage. We model the Image of God.** The fact that there's only one person trying to manage the home (actually micromanage a lot of things) means they're limited, as singles. If the mom has to work from 10 in the morning until 8 at night, you're talking about a gap of probably three hours where the kid's at home alone. They're already stuck with a huge problem.

They need some help. They need to call on some others for some help like good youth groups. And let the youth ministry be something like what you, Ron, called a "City of Refuge," in an earlier *Youthworker* article. Steve Sjogren, a pastor out of Cincinnati, has a whole thing called "Conspiracy of Kindness." His church is really committed to helping single parents have fun, have a night out, and to provide them some babysitting. They even do what is called a "single parent oil change," where approximately once a month they sponsor a free oil and filter change for single parents. So, I think that single parents need to know their limits — what they're good at, what they're not good at — and then call out for some help. They're going to need support.

Wayne Rice

First of all, **don't think you have to get remarried** in order to provide your kid with what they need, because it may be in the best interest of your kid for you to stay single. **The blended family is often worse off than the single parent family.** Second, I'd say get in a good church with a good youth group, so your kids have the benefit of that kind of support. Third, **surround your kid with as many adult mentors as possible. Adults who can interact with them, who can teach and love your kids almost as much as you do.**

Thom Schultz

I would say never, never, never discount God's design of the powerful influence of *both* a mom *and* a dad in a kid's life. Even if it's in some less-than-ideal setting. If both influences aren't abundantly present in a kid's life, get them. One of the obvious ways to help single parents is through mentors. If you don't have a mentor for your kid, ask your church to set up a mentor program. I think more and more research shows the power of mentoring. I read something yesterday for an issue of *Group* magazine: **Kids in a Big Brother/Big Sister program are 46% less likely to start using drugs than kids who don't have a mentor, but want one.** Many kids are waiting in line for a mentor. They realize the value of it, but they haven't found one yet.

RH: How does the church provide serious guides for teens who need mentors?

TS: There are some good models for setting up mentoring programs. Oftentimes these models involve a lot of people in the church who ordinarily haven't found a place to fit in because they've felt, "I can't do that. I can't do that." But if mentoring basically means being a friend to somebody else, there are scores of people who say, "Well, I can do that!" **I was a member of a church a few years ago that was not a large church, probably a Sunday attendance of 250-300. But we had ninety adults involved in the**

youth ministry program, and the vast majority of those were mentors. They're only job was simply to be a friend to one of the teenagers in the church. It worked!

RH: Off the top of your head can you think of a resource, a book, or a video that helps parents to that end — that helps adults in churches to be mentors?

TS: The resource that Miles McPherson and Wayne Rice produced, called *One Kid At a Time*, is excellent!

Les Parrott

One thing I would stress is that divorce or death in the marriage doesn't end a family. **According to my statistics, over one out of five of all families are currently single parent families, and that's the fastest growing family form in the United States. No other type of family has increased so rapidly.**

RH: Where's that statistic from?

LP: From my new book, called *Once Upon a Family*, published by Beacon Hill. A single-parent family is not a two-parent family with one parent temporarily absent. **The message that I would want to convey to these families is that I would want to encourage them.** They somehow feel like they are at a disadvantage. I don't necessarily agree with that. I think there are definite obstacles that they're going to have to work harder at overcoming, but **some research has even shown that kids in single parent homes tend to be more responsible. They have to learn to make up for some things that other families might take for granted.** But you know, in spite of any positive things, there are definitely some struggles they're going to encounter.

Furthermore, they must realize they're still a family. That they've got a challenge. And that they're not alone in that challenge. They're going to need to pay particular attention to some of the gender issues of their adolescents. If it's a single mom, she's going to need to make sure that those kids have some male role models — some healthy male role models — and vice versa.

Ken Davis

Get help! Single parents, as well as all parents, need to take advantage of every resource available to them. In the past, parents — including single parents — had the help of their extended family. But in today's society, where the literal family often lives hundreds and hundreds of miles away, it is very important for them to establish an extended family. That's were I believe that the church is so valuable, not only for providing instruction for singles, but for finding other people who care for your kids — someone willing to mentor your children along with you. People who are willing to help you in such a way that it also gives you the necessary time to be a parent with your kids. **That's the one thing I would say more than anything else: not to go at it alone, but to really engage other people in your parenting responsibilities.**

Harold Ivan Smith

Some of the great heroes and heroines of our culture these days are single parents. I'm very concerned about some of the cheap shots that politicians and millionaires take on single parents. Last year 34 billion dollars in child support was collected. It is estimated that 800,000 women could leave welfare, if their former spouse paid alimony and child support. I see so many parents who are trying to do the impossible with little money, little resources, little encouragement, and — occasionally from the church — only a little patronizing pat on the head, "My, you're doing such a good job with your kids."

I tell them that they don't have to be "perfect parents," only "good enough parents." I hope they will not get involved in things "to prove what a great parent I am, and this child will rise up and call me blessed." Because if you do that, the child won't rise up and call you blessed. The child will call you everything but blessed. **There needs to be the sense that "I can't be both the mother and the father, but I can be the good parent, whether I'm the father or the mother. I can do the best job I can, and trust that the rest is the grace of God."**

I remember one evangelist screaming at her two children, "You're not going to have a teenage crisis. There's not going to be any teenage rebellion. I will not permit it!" The scarring it did to those children really troubles me. Because she was a single parent, suddenly she was trying to prove something to the world: "My children will be perfect. They *will* be perfect." It's very unfortunate to put that kind of pressure on them. Look for resources that will help you, but also nurture yourself as a single parent, because if you don't have it within you, you don't have it to give out. **I see lots of parents that run on very low batteries all the time.**

RH: How do they nurture themselves, in particular?

HS: I think by reading: having a strong spiritual life is very important. It's easy, late at night to grab a Bible and read a verse of Scripture — **in essence, you "had devotions" — but you've not had a devotional life.** That parent has to find quality time alone, even if it's only ten minutes. It's a time for them to admit to God, "I need your help. You have got to help me. You have got to befriend me as I'm single parenting." Then look for solid places where there are programs that assist the needs of single parents.

Rick Dunn

Respect them. Then tell them they're making a difference. Even if you (as a single parent) feel limited, it does make a difference to your kid that you care. One study I read showed that, while quantity time is important, what is most important is the perception of the child: that, if you — as a parent — were given the opportunity to take time to be with them, they perceive that you would do that. And that is a huge finding.

Most of the Christian literature addresses the parent who has custody of the kid, not the parent who doesn't. And there are many Christian mothers and fathers who don't have their children living with them. Those parents tend to get judged, so they need a lot of support and affirmation. Even if they are the "weekend dad" or the "weekend mom," they are huge in that young person's life. Obviously, they grieve because they can't have more, but what they are doing still makes a difference.

Another critical situation is the scenario when the early adolescent begins to idealize what a parent should be and what a family should be. And the parent that they dump on is not the person they don't get to see; it's the one they have to live with everyday. So they unrealistically start wanting to live with that other, absent parent. A lot of single parents don't know that is coming, and they are not prepared for it.

Lastly, a caution: don't have your kid as your primary confidant or friend. It may be tempting if you have a fourteen year old who is sympathetic to make him or her your best buddy. But you really need a peer or mentor to do that.

Dennis McCluen

I say: **"You are not a bad parent, but you have a tougher job than people who have a spouse." That is not a condemning statement; it's a reality statement.** The first step is to be honest with them about that. Not defensive. Not blaming. Single parents have a tougher job. There is a piece missing. Studies show that that is a significant piece. To pretend that is not true or to assume that they alone can replace that piece is a mistake. They have to be honest with themselves and find some support from the intergenerational faith community, neighbors, and friends. Lastly I would say, "Don't give up." Even though they have a tougher job, some single parents are doing a great job, often better than some intact family because many have a plan. They are going after their kids and getting their needs met. They are not letting the kids do the parenting. They have maintained the parental role.

The church has often missed a great opportunity to support and encourage and assist those single parents in a way that is not condemning. The church can't assume that single parents have the same needs as a dual parent family. They have to go after them. They have to figure out what the single parents in their church need. For some, it is a financial need; for some, it is relational; for some, it is simply babysitting.

Chapter 7
What Your Teen Needs to Hear

If given the chance to speak with the adolescents themselves, what would you say to them — about their parents — which would strengthen the home?

Ken Davis

I did that in my book, *How to Live with Your Parents without Losing Your Mind.* **Basically, for youth to understand that their parents are not against them.** Let their parents make mistakes. I tell parents not to put themselves on a pedestal, but I think that kids often put their parents on a pedestal. And that doesn't allow them to make mistakes.

The other thing I would say is that kids have an unbelievable potential for making an impact in

Kids have an unbelievable potential to impact their homes.

their homes. But they'll never see it done if their major concern is: "What can I get out of it?" **In the eighteen years that I spent in my home, I can't remember thirty seconds that I ever, ever woke up thinking, "What can I do for my parents today that would really** make their day easier?" or "What can I do to make this a great day today for my parents?" **Kids have an unbelievable potential to impact their homes.**

Haman Cross

I would share personal experiences. **If you go to the doctor and you tell him what is wrong, he writes out a prescription. I really believe that God knows exactly what is wrong with a kid.**

So He prescribes the exact parents that they are to have. He did not ask the kid for their input on it. These parents are prescribed, and that is the best thing for those children, including personality differences and all that stuff. It's a great, great preparation for their life. If they have a mother or father that they can't get along with because of conflicting personalities, this concept is still great preparation for their lives. They have to see their life and faith that way. And make the best of it.

> We have lost the sense of God's sovereignty and His purpose.

We have lost the sense of God's sovereignty and His purpose. We've forgotten that God will raise up a family, a nation, an individual. He will prepare them. He may use weird ways (to us). **But we need to give kids a sense of destiny. It will help them make sense of biblical characters' lives like Joseph. Like him, we may have to make some pit stops. But he ended up in Egypt and he maintained who he was. God's sovereignty was there. And I think that kids can grasp that concept earlier than we think.**

Dennis McCluen

I try to tell them there are four things that are true about their parents. **First, parents are untrained for the job that they have.** They aren't prepared for the job daily appearing in front of their eyes. I help kids realize that. Second, they are tired from the world they live in. Most parents that I have talked to are tired, physically.

> Parents are untrained for the job that they have.

They are also tired of not having easy answers. They are tired of the never-ending nature of parenting. Third, I tell them that **most parents are scared.** They are really fearful of what might happen with all the options available to teens. **When you are fearful you act kind of weird.** The fourth piece I tell kids is that **every parent that I have ever talked to loves their kids beyond anything those kids could ever understand.** They may not act like they love teens sometimes — that is one of the critical problems, that parents don't act like they love them — but they do.

Ron Habermas: I wonder if there is some simulation game that you can use with teens to teach those four truths. For example, simulate an experience in a teen's life that identifies something that they, too, are untrained for: where they are stressed out; when they're scared; where they love someone. Start out with that simulation game, and then talk about the implications of parenting.

DM: I think that's a good idea, because those characteristics are true for them, and they relate to being tired and untrained and acting weird.

Dan Bautista

Last fall, my daughter realized something profound about me. She came to realize that I have the same needs and the same wants (in many ways) that she has. For example, friendship. Sometimes we present to teenagers the idea that parents don't need anybody or anything. Even in our work as missionaries and in church leadership roles, sometimes we live as though we don't have anyone that we're close to. She has just realized in the last few months that she wants friends, and that I want friends, too. **I long for friendships, just as she does.**

When we moved down from Columbia, South Carolina to Texas I was missing my friend JJ and missing some of the subjects that we talked about. **When she told me that she was missing her friend and started crying, I told her that I also missed JJ and her reaction was like: "Wow! I didn't know you could feel the same thing!"**

129

RH: What has that done for your relationship with her?

DB: She's now looking at me through a more human perspective. We can talk a little more openly about these things. **We parents do have needs. We're not as all-powerful and almighty as we pretend to be.**

Les Parrott

The same message that I would give to the parents, just reversed: learn to empathize. Learn to put yourself in your parents' shoes. Then, when parents make seemingly unrealistic or irrational requests, you understand a little bit of where that's coming from. Recognize their anxiety. When you do that, your understanding will bring more peace to your own spirit about why your parents do the things they do. That's the answer. How you would phrase that advice to teens, however, is very different than you would to their parents.

Harold Ivan Smith

I say: "Cut them some slack. They are human. You have to understand that your parents are fearful (or maybe anxious is a better word). They are trying to love you in a culture that's very difficult to love teens. And many of them are doing the best that they can. Sometimes you just have to understand the struggle that your parents have. They want the best for you. But they see many things that cause them to be anxious and that makes it very difficult for them to be the kind of parent that many teenagers want."

RH: You say it's difficult to love teens sometimes in this culture. Is there anything that the teens themselves could do, to lay off some habits, perhaps, or to emphasize some positive things?

HS: One is trying to hear where your parents are coming from. Don't resort to guilting your parents: "John's parents are going to let him do that." Sometimes you use those subtle influences that become wedges between fathers and mothers. **It's very tempting, as a teen, to learn how to manipulate;** to realize what am I pretending not to know about the choices I'm making. That I am manipulating my parents. What I find is the stakes get bigger. They start off very small, like: "Can I stay up until 10 o'clock?" Then the stakes escalate because you get very good at learning how to manipulate your parents. That can become a lifelong habit.

RH: How about codependency in the home? Some parents seem to get off on that, in a very twisted kind of way, too.

HS: Very much so. Sometimes they don't want their teens to make mistakes or to learn from the mistakes. They want to rush in and bail the kid out. One of the greatest experiences my dad ever gave me was at Christmas back in '64, when I had a car wreck. He said, "You're into this. You're going to have to get yourself out of it." He said, "You're going to the State Farm agent yourself. You're going to deal with this issue. You're the one driving the car." I was pretty irritated, saying, "Don't you want to go with me?" He said, "Who was driving the car?" "Well, I was driving the car." "All right, then you're going to have to deal with it." It was an incredible responsibility, but there wasn't another wreck. I learned that. What I had learned from that experience made me a much better driver. And I'm sure it would have been very easy for him to say, "I'm coming with you." He really made me accept the responsibility for what had happened. He made me bear the full weight of my actions.

RH: Which is an incredible legacy to give any teenager.

HS: Right. And I wasn't happy about it at the time. I don't need to say that.

Helen Musick

When you stand up before teens, you can't be profound. I think you can tell stories from your childhood and your adolescence that they can relate to. That's what I do. I try to tell them stories of what happened in my life during adolescence. And how I thought my parents were out of touch; they didn't understand what I felt like. Only to find out, now that I'm not a teenager anymore, that my parents *did* understand.

RH: So, you'd hope to convey what kinds of truths with the stories?

HM: I'd say to them that their parents, with years of experience, have wisdom that they don't have. That they need to trust them. If it is a healthy parent situation, then I would say that. **Their parents basically do the best that they can. At some point, the kids have got to accept that.**

Mark Senter

I have yet to meet the parent that hates her or his children, even in abusive homes. Typically, the parent really does love their child. They might have such bad patterns of responding to tense situations that they need to deal with that. But parents really do love teens. Kids need to have that perspective before they go judging their parents.

The second thing I'd say to youth in a theological context, (maybe I should put this first) is that God called you to this family. Learn what you can from your situation. That's not the kind of thing you say when a kid comes in struggling but it's part of the teaching — or the preventive work — of the church.

Teach them that God called them and placed them within that family. The greatness of God, the providence of God. Let me illustrate from my own experience. My mom was a manic depressive. By the time I was nine years of age she was in a mental hospital. From that time until she died, she was in and out of hospitals. **Our family was probably dysfunctional by most standards because we were coping with my mom's condition for the rest of our lives. But God called me to that family. Who I am today is dependent not on what Mom did, but what God did in my life in the process of being part of that family.** That captures what I would like to tell kids.

> *Our family was probably dysfunctional ... but God called me to that family.*

RH: The faith community has stories to tell that teens need to hear. Youth need to be aware of the other people that sit in the pew down from them. There are stories all around them of God's work "in spite of."

MS: Well said. In our day and time, that's extremely important.

Mark Cannister

It would be pretty profound if teenagers understood that their parents actually love them. Many years ago, J.B. Phillips wrote a book called *Your God Is Too Small.* You could write the same kind of book about parents. A lot of teenagers look at parents as the disciplinarian, the judge who's sitting on the bench, who's always coming down on them. Other teenagers look at the parent as the auto mechanic

It would be pretty profound if teenagers understood that their parents actually loved them.

who is there to fix whatever goes wrong. Other teenagers look at the parent as Santa Claus who's there to provide for their every need. I think **teenagers have a very single-minded view of parents. And we need to tell them that parents really do love them in a very holistic way.**

Len Kageler

Kids don't often think that their parents have ever been as old as they are. Most kids think that when you're an adult, your problems sort of level out. You know, you get a job, you get married, you get a car and a stereo and a TV and a decent house. That pretty well is it. But kids need to know that the lives of adults — their parents — can be filled with betrayal, loss, nasty surprises, unfairness, and troubling things. Their world is hard, and I know it's very hard for a kid to understand it. To a kid who's also experiencing life's difficulties for the first time as an adolescent, it seems all-encompassing.

RH: So, how do you convey that to the teen? A series of lectures?

LK: Lecturing is really never the best approach to communicate anything to kids. You could develop a role play situation where you give the kids a chance to act out parental problems. For example, one thing that kids deal with is gossip. In a church youth ministry situation, getting them to simulate that might be good. Like this role: as an adult, you've just overheard the person in the cubicle next to you say that they heard someone call you an alcoholic. What are you going to do? It's unfair; it's untrue. It's potentially damaging to your career, your reputation, to everything that's dear to you. Teens could easily see how powerful that would be. Kids don't think that parents experience these problems. So, simulation is one possible way to get at this information and empathy.

David Olshine

I'd say to teenagers that **I'd like for them to switch roles with their parents for one week. I'd like teens to have one week in their parents' shoes. I'd like the kids to be up earlier than their parents. I'd like them to do all of the meals. I'd like them to do all the shopping. I'd like them to drive the parents to work. I'd like them to pick the parents up. I'd like them to reverse the whole thing. I want them to do the laundry and cut the grass. And, at the end of the week, see if they aren't a little bit more grateful.**

Teens in our culture are spoiled. I've got a number of international students at my university who absolutely honor their parents. They are so grateful for what their parents have done. And some of them are very poor. I think that, in the American culture, teenagers are spoiled rotten — most of them. I'm thinking of Caucasian, middle-class kids who have turned their parents off. They think that their parents owe them everything. They're disrespectful. The way to get their attention is to tell them to reverse the roles for a while.

Leith Anderson

All the research shows that parents are clearly the most influential people in their adolescent's life. That just stuns parents because they don't think that is true. They think that their kids' peers are. I guess the best thing that would be helpful to children, as they move to be teenagers, would be to say, "Yes, your parents are important. No, they are not perfect, and here are five things that you can do to benefit from your parents. **Benefit from your parents, don't reject." If all children could learn that, they could really grow through some tough years.**

Roger Cross

Help kids understand the pressures that their parents face. I would start out with a group of kids talking about the incredible pressures *they* face. Let them identify those pressures, then let them say, "Man, we've got a lot of pressures." Finally, I'd say, "Now, let's talk about your parents. Do they have any pressures?" **My experience has been, when we get to this question, most kids don't have a clue. They've never even thought about their parents having any pressures.** But when you begin to identify their parents' pressures (and you really have to lead them), they begin to see. It gives them a little more understanding of what their parents are facing. For example, to help a kid see that their dad has this incredible pressure at work to produce. When he comes home, sometimes he's somber, nonresponsive, and exhausted. Teens need to know where those responses are coming from.

Jay Kesler

All kids say first of all, "My parents don't trust me." And I say to them, "This is a two-way street. You have got to communicate with your parents enough that they know where you're at, so that they realize you're worthy of trust. **Parents will give you trust when they feel you're worthy of trust. There's no way they can know you're worthy unless you discuss your values with them, unless your parents know where you're at on certain issues.** Instead of just speaking to parents in low grunts and moans and raised eyebrows, if you will tell them your values, tell them how you feel about certain things, they will tend to give you pieces of trust. If you don't abuse that, then you will become trustworthy."

135

I am always pleased, here at Taylor University when, in a case of discipline, the parent comes and takes the side of the kid, saying, "Well, Jay, I tend to believe what he says because I have a lifetime experience of trusting him." I don't take that lightly when a parent tells me that. On the other hand, if the parent has been indulgent and doesn't really know the kid and is kind of overprotective, he may say, "I can trust him." Then I ask, "How can you trust him?" Because there's no precedent for testing that trust. Then I realize that's just a doting parent who's naive.

There's a way for a kid to build trust in the home where the dad or mom will go to the wall for him. That's a beautiful thing. But it's largely the responsibility of the teenager to convey. The larger privileges of tomorrow are dependent on the smaller things you do today. And I keep trying to help kids see that connection because they tend to think all the little stuff is just junk. Yet, someday, they say, "I want to have a car." They've got to learn that Dad gives you the car when you show him that you can handle the family's pet rabbit.

Marlene LeFever

If you, as a teen, are going through a struggle, know for a fact that your parents are going through the same struggle, only flipside. For example: you're learning what it means to be a sexual human being; you're excited about your sexuality. Your parent is at the age where he or she may be a little worried about their own sexuality. Or, you're thinking, as a teenager, how exciting it is to be going into your first job. Your parents, on the flipside, are watching all these young turks coming up through the ranks — who know more about technology than they do — and they're a little worried about how long it will be before someone takes over their position. **Kids don't think about the fact that their parents are going through pretty identical, parallel challenges, but twenty years removed.**

RH: Are you trying to build empathy, to build awareness?

ML: I don't know if a teen is capable of being empathetic towards a parent. That might be asking too much of her age level. But at least teens can know that being an adult has its challenges that go beyond their own experiences, and yet are similar to theirs.

Dave Rahn

Just a very practical piece of advice: **"Treat your parents today like you want to remember, when you're together at Christmas — with them — ten years from now."** It's the wider perspective that's the important one to keep urging teens to envision. The long term perspective. They get so short-focused on the points of disagreement and conflict. They often rage about tonight's curfew, or hair styles, or those kinds of things.

RH: That problem seems to go both ways. Parents are short-focused, too.

DR: I think so. But the task for the teen — and this is a word that I might not use because it's a turn-off word — **the task of a teen is to submit.** That mature attitude will enable them to say: "Yeah, I'm open to considering that my parents might be right" and "There's stuff I can do right now to change my behaviors, so that I have a good relationship in the long haul."

RH: Anything else?

DR: I think communication is a very difficult thing for parents of teens. So teens can really grease the skids, by seeking open communication with their own parents.

Wayne Rice

That parents are a lot like them. They have emotions, they get hurt, they're struggling with their self-image, they get mad, and they do the wrong thing sometimes. I tell this to parents, too, because the reverse is also true. I tell them to remember when they were a teenager. If they can remember, then maybe that will help their relationship a little bit. I tell teenagers that their parents really aren't that much different than them, in a lot of important ways. Sure they dress funny, and they focus on a lot of different concerns. **Teens are concerned about their zits, parents are concerned**

about the economy. So, I tell youth to try to understand that their folks are human beings. They make mistakes, too.

Mike Yaconelli

First of all, teens can't understand them. Not totally. But they can understand some things. One is that their parents need affirmation. I'd say, "When was the last time you, as a kid, wrote your mom and dad a note and said, 'I love you guys. You guys are cool. Thank you for all you do for me'? **When was the last time that you cleaned *their* room when *they* were out for a few hours shopping? When was the last time you fixed them breakfast in bed?** I mean there are so many little creative things you can do, as a kid, to say, 'You are so cool. I love you. Thank you for all you do.'" **Many kids are so into themselves. It's just part of adolescence. So inward that they can't see outward.**

And it just takes a few suggestions. Here's something that you can do. Here's a little thing that will make a huge difference in your parents' lives. It goes a long way. Little things, like when teens come back from camp — to show that they met God at camp — and none of them have anything to do with reading their Bible. They're real practical, like: don't use the phone for a week; don't play any music for a week; those kinds of things. So there's plenty that kids can do to recognize that Mom and Dad need some encouragement and some help. There are some things that they can do, without being asked, that make a huge difference in the tension of adolescence and becoming independent and growing up.

Thom Schultz

I tell teenagers that their parents are made of the same stuff they are.

Kids and parents both struggle. They both doubt. Both make mistakes. Both experience guilt. They both hide their true feelings from time to time. If we all understand that, then the next — and most important — step is to forgive and seek forgiveness.

"What would you say to adolescents about their parents?"

Rick Dunn

I say to them that the biggest mistake their parents will make will come out of their love for them. This does not mean they should uncritically accept their mistakes, but it may help them absorb faults a little bit better. They need to understand that, when somebody desperately and deeply loves someone, they could be scared or overly concerned.

Secondly, **expect failures.** And **realize that grace is something that needs to be shared both ways.** You want your parents to deal with you in grace, so also learn to be gracious towards your parents. That is a part of our Christian walk. To minister grace to one another. Genuine Christian grace. And this is a hard application to some older adolescents. I say to them, "Don't burn bridges no matter how difficult it may be. Because, **when it is all said and done, your parents are the people you are going to come back to one day."**

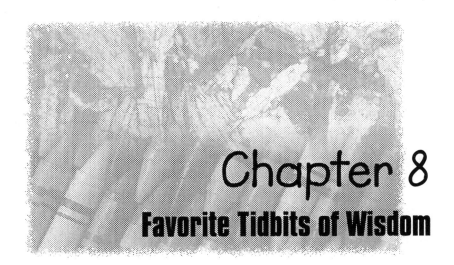

Chapter 8
Favorite Tidbits of Wisdom

Is there any particular story, or humorous saying, or quotable quote that keeps you focused on the essence of what parenting teens is all about?

Marlene LeFever

A couple of weeks ago, my husband and I had a Japanese girl in our home. She wanted an American experience, and so her tour group gave her one overnight and two days in an American home. We told her one of the things that we always did was go to church. And she was thrilled, because she said that she and her family were Buddhists, and she'd never been inside a Christian church. She was excited about going.

So we went, and I listened to the church service through what I thought were her eyes and her ears. I liked what she saw, but I wondered how on earth she would understand what she heard because we have so many clichés. At the end of the service, I asked if there was anything that she wanted explained. She said no, she had pretty much understood everything. A woman, during the service, had given her testimony, and the Japanese girl sort of struggled with her vocabulary, as she recalled it. But she finally came out with

For someone to say: "Here's a church woman that gets excited about her Jesus."

an incredible summary reaction: "That church mother sure got excited about her Jesus person." I like that line. **I want people to be able to see by my life and my actions — that "here's a church women that gets excited about her Jesus."** That irreplaceable enthusiasm of being a Christian is often difficult for us to show.

Mark Cannister

Yogi Berra has lots of great quotes, and one of his was, "It ain't over 'til it's over." Life is a process. Caring for teenagers is a process, and parents and youth pastors need to remember it isn't over until it's over. Especially when it looks like it's really going down the tubes. **This week may be horrible, but next week may be great. You never know what's going to happen in the bottom of the ninth inning of a teenager's life.**

Dave Rahn

I have a picture in my mind of some of the warmest times in my home, as an adolescent. At least three of us were teens, and we'd get into a King of the Couch contest with my parents. I wasn't raised in a home where love was freely expressed verbally, but those experiences were expressions of comfort for me. **Home was a comfortable place to be. And we had comfortable relationships. To be able to say that about a home, during the teenage years, is a wonderful tribute. It's one that I really aspire to. I want my home to always be comfortable to my kids and their friends. In fact, that's the way I measure** whether or not my home is comfortable: if a teenage daughter or son is able to bring their friends home. I want to do that.

The way I measure success: if my teenage daughter or son is able to bring their friends home.

"Is there anything that keeps you focused on what it's all about?"

Ken Davis

The only thing I can think of right now is **"If you don't succeed the first time, blame your parents." That's real fashionable right now.**

Harold Ivan Smith

I'll tell a little story about a young man, a friend who was dying of AIDS. He had been dismissed from the hospital in South Florida because Hurricane Andrew was coming in. He was going to be forced to go through the hurricane alone, so he called his father and asked: "Would you come and ride out the hurricane with me?" So what you saw on CNN was that incredible rush of traffic out of South Florida keys and the Miami/Fort Lauderdale area. You saw the bumper to bumper traffic going north. You did *not* see the car going south, the father trying to get to his son. He went into a boarded up house, prepared for the storm.

In the middle of the night, when the electricity went off, the air conditioning went off, the son could not breathe. So his father carried him out to the car and ran the car motor, in order for him to use the air conditioner. The part of South Florida that they were in saw the storm pass. It didn't hit the area. So he carried his son back in, restored the house and eventually went home. But after his son died, I asked the father, "Why did you do that? Why did you put yourself in harm's way, in real danger, when you could have ridden out the storm in the house?" **And I'll never forget what he said, "I didn't want my boy to die without him knowing how much I loved him."**

It ties back to what I meant about expressed love. There was never any doubt, as that young man died, how deep his father's love was for him.

It goes back to what I think Samuel 14:14 teaches: God devises ways so that the banished do not feel estranged from Him. I think that's talking about King David reaching out to his son. But it's also about how God is working to devise a way so His children can come back to relationship with Him. That's what many parents

143

have to do these days, when sons and daughters — of whatever age — have disappointed and wounded them. **It would be wonderful if the prodigal son story could be read over and over in families, so that it's such a deep part of each household's values.**

> It would be wonderful if the prodigal son story could be read over and over in families, so that it's such a deep part of each household's values.

I remember one other story. There was a movie called the Emerald Forest. In it, a young blond kid wandered away from a construction camp in Brazil and was taken by Indian tribes. What I learned from the movie was based upon the father, a construction worker, who went out every weekend to search in those jungles, looking for his son. I invited my two godsons and their father over for dinner one Saturday night and we watched it. We watched this very intense movie together. When they went home, in the dark of the car, the older son (who was then 13) leaned forward and said, **"Dad, would you go that far if I was lost? Would you come and look for me?"** And he said, "Well, Denny, I sure would." That movie, with all of the five of us watching it, became an incredible moment for the father to express his love: "Yes I would. I would do whatever I had to do to try to find you." There's an example of watching a movie that talks about the family commitment. It says a lot to the young man who says, "Yeah, my dad would be willing to go that far." It's very important that we see those realities. **That was important for Denny to hear. That was a story that he needed to hear.** For his father to conclude: "Yes, I would do all of that to try to find you if you were lost."

Thom Schultz

Parents and youth workers today need to have a long term vision of youth ministry and of parenting. I cringe now, thinking about everything my parents put up with with me when I was a kid. But they had long term vision. Our back yard back then was, half of the time, filled with carnivals. I'd build rides and all sorts of stuff. The front yards were filled with lemonade stands. I even built a ferris wheel one time in the front yard — an actual operating ferris wheel! A lot of people were stopping. I remember one time I wanted to get a crowd for one of my shows, and my parents were off at work, so I hung a sign on the garage door (and our house stood on a main thoroughfare). **I put up this huge sign — the size of the garage door itself — with three huge letters on it: S-E-X, in big red letters.** Then, in tiny letters that you would have to walk up to in order to see, it said, "Now that I have your attention, there's a big carnival show in my basement today at 2:00." My parents came home and saw that sign. You can imagine seeing this huge SEX symbol on the door! But they were good about it.

Ron Habermas: How old were you?

TS: I was probably 12 or 13. **My parents had a long term vision for me. They allowed my creativity to develop. They saw that my creativity was more important than a tidy house or some bizarre escapades.**

Roger Cross

That more is *caught* than *taught*. That doesn't minimize teaching in a traditional sense, but the best teaching is what kids see. What you model.

RH: Which gets back to the matter of time. Though it is different for kids than for teens, there's the particular need to just be there for your children.

RC: I think that's what Deuteronomy 6 is all about: when you're going and when you're coming. They're seeing you. When your kids are riding with you on the freeway and a guy cuts you off, you're going to teach your child something by your response.

Les Parrott

I prefer the quote by DeWitt Talmage: "A church within a church, a republic within a republic, a world within a world, is

spelled in four letters: H-O-M-E." If things go right there, they go right everywhere. I think that most of us involved in youth ministry today understand that it's not just ministry to those kids, but it's ministry to that home. That's not a light statement.

Len Kageler

We have a couple of sayings around our house. **I often say, "The Kingdom will probably go on." That is, the Kingdom of God somehow surges ahead, even when we get a setback. Another line we often say around our house is, "Well, it's not the bubonic plague, is it?"** We've tried to instill in our kids those little bits of history. Like one time, when we lived in Seattle, I was reading a book on plagues and people. In most communities back then, 60% of the people died. So, I took my children (they were just elementary students) around our block and said, "Well, in the year 1350, in the last ten houses that we just passed, there would only be people alive in four of them." That really impacted them. This kind of experience puts the fact that they are confused about a boyfriend or a girl-friend in a proper perspective. At least it does for an adolescent who's more mature; one who can think abstractly.

> *Another line we often say around our house is, "Well, it's not the bubonic plague, is it?"*

Mark Senter

I've never been able to get away from Harold Garner's statement at Moody Bible Institute, **"Love 'em and feed 'em."** I believe that's a lot of the process of working with kids: loving and feeding them. Both the physical food — lots of it — and secondly, nurturing kind of food. Beyond that, I would have to say, "Hang in there." **Serving youth, like police work, is 98% boring. The other 2% is raw adrenaline rush,** where you are saying, "Wow, where did I come up

> *Serving youth, like police work, is 98% boring. The other 2% is raw adrenaline rush.*

"Is there anything that keeps you focused on what it's all about?"

with the resource to do that?" But suddenly you have to do something, and you're in the right place at the right time. And the reason you're there is because of the other 98% of what you were doing. So, it's the "hang in there" advice.

Jay Kesler

The goal of parenthood is developing independence in the child. That can be tremendously threatening for parents. Oftentimes the parent — though they intellectually know that they're supposed to be developing a self-reliant, self-regulating young adult — has inadvertently built their psychological needs around the child's dependence. So there are two things happening at once. While the child is growing to independence — the ability to monitor their own young adult life — the parent has to also be growing psychologically and emotionally to the place that they can take pride in their own independence from the child, **their ability to make it on their own. This is the core to the parent-teen struggle. That's why I believe in resident colleges, and kids going away to college. It's kind of a decompression chamber, to a degree.**

I use the illustration of the wren. The young wren eventually flies away from the rest by taking little loops away from the nest, enlarging the loops until they come to build their own nest. I don't know their behavior well enough to know if they come back and talk to the mother about their own nest or not. But, if parents don't let their kids take these ever enlarging loops during childhood and early adolescence, to see them take "one great migration" into the army or into the workplace — it can't be done. They've got to take the little loops. They've got to have the week away at grandma's house; they've got to have the two weeks at camp; they've got to have the overnighter with the boy scouts. They've got to have the job where they're required by their boss to be there — where someone else is holding them accountable. They've got to handle these little experiences so that they can handle the big ones. **A lot of parents seem unwilling or unable to give them these separating experiences. They take care of everything because of their own**

147

adult needs. **This is the great sin, really, of the evangelical parents. In fact, I think the evangelical parents probably do better with younger children, compared with the general population. But I think they do less well with adolescents.** They get frightened when their kids get a little older and, in a sense, don't trust themselves. I try to help parents get great doses of self-confidence.

In the early years of parenting, you're putting money in the bank as it were — "equity" — and then you draw it out in middle and late adolescence.

Rick Dunn

So we shouldn't strive to be perfect, we should strive to be redemptive.

This is a Ted Ward saying that he told me once: If you take a perfect institution and you go there, it won't be perfect anymore. That's a good thing to remember: **There is no perfect family. There is no ideal. So we shouldn't strive to be perfect, we should strive to be redemptive.** We are going to mess up. We are going to disappoint each other. We are going to get mad. We are going to sin. And we don't need to cover that over; we don't need to ignore it; we just need to deal with it redemptively. That's what a healthy family is.

Leith Anderson

"This too shall pass." This part of your life is only one chapter. It's not the whole story.

Helen Musick

I was thinking of a story of a girl that lived next door to me. She would come over to my house and hang out a lot. She was fifteen and wanted to get her ears pierced. The story, for me, defines adolescence. She went to her mother and asked if she could get her ears pierced. And her mother said, like a lot of moms say, "Go ask your dad. It's okay with me, but go ask your dad." **So the teen** went to ask her dad if she could get her ears pierced and her dad said, "If God meant for you to have holes in your ears, then you'd be born with them." And this fifteen year old said to her father, "Oh, well, how did you get that tattoo on your arm?" And he sent her to her room and grounded her for the rest of the weekend.

What I love about that story is that it, first of all, really describes what is happening with teenagers, when they're fourteen and fifteen with regard to the shift from concrete to abstract thinking. This young girl was able to come to her father with a rational question that was making comparisons with abstract, formal thinking. For the father, however, that was very threatening to his parenting style. We all make mistakes and say things we shouldn't say. But what I would have counseled him to do is to go up to his daughter and say, "I responded in the wrong way. Your ability to make that kind of comparison threatened me. And the reason I acted so strongly is that I made my decision at age seventeen. I have to live with that decision on my arm for the rest of my life. Ears pierced isn't the same as a tattoo, but that's how I see it and I wish I hadn't done it. If you want to pierce your ears, after a week of thinking about it, go ahead."

David Olshine

The only thing that comes to my mind is a quote by our friend, Wayne Rice: **"Rules without relationship leads to rebellion."** And I'd like to add another axiom: **"Relationship without some rules leads to anarchy."** If a parent is continually pushing their kid, lifting that symbolic bar so high that the kid has to keep jumping higher, eventually that kid is going to get deflated and not be able to succeed. I think of the movie *Dead Poets' Society*, where one boy keeps "jumping" and can't jump any higher, since his father keeps lifting the bar when his kid's down. The other family extreme is "no rules," where the film *Mrs. Doubtfire* is a good example. Initially, there are no rules in their family. There's an opening scene with a party going on. Everybody's dancing. There are horses in the house eating the birthday cake. Those movies are two extremes. One is a rigid system and one is a chaotic system. And I see that a lot in the culture. So, I'd say, "balance rules and relationships."

I want a lifetime relationship with my daughter Rachel. We're not talking short term here. We're not talking just getting through seven years, which is the way a lot of people look at it — they've just got to get through the turbulence of adolescence. Well, you are going to get through the turbulence. You're going to land the plane, but the question is, how safely will you land it? I like that analogy of the airplane. We are going to have turbulence in teenage years. But the question is, "How much damage will be done to the plane?" I want a lifelong journey. Adult to adult. I don't view it as the next three or four years with Rachel. I view it as "where will I be at 65 or 75 years old? And where will she be? What will our relationship look like, then?"

Mike Yaconelli

One story I use all the time is from Robert Fulghum, in his book *All I Really Needed to Know I Learned in Kindergarten.* It's a story about how he had seventy or eighty kids that he had to take care of for an hour. So, he decided to play Giants, Wizards, and Dwarfs. It's kind of like Rock, Paper, and Scissors. Everybody runs around and becomes a giant, a wizard, or a dwarf. A giant beats a wizard, a wizard beats a dwarf, or a dwarf beats a giant. He explained the game to them, got them all wound up, let them run around for a while, and then yelled out, "Giants, Wizards, Dwarfs!" All the kids begin pairing up and becoming one or the other. Then Fulghum feels a little tug at his pantleg. He looks down and there's a little five-year-old girl, with big blue eyes staring up at him. She asks him, "Um, where do the mermaids go?" He says, "There's no such thing as mermaids," and she says, "Yes, there is; I'm a mermaid." Then he said, "For the next 45 minutes, I held hands with a mermaid, while everyone else became a giant, wizard, or a dwarf."

Our job is to say to teens, "The culture says that you can only be a giant, wizard, or a dwarf." But they're wrong. When

you meet Jesus, you discover that there are a whole lot of things that you can be that no one ever thought of before. That is the joy of what we do.

RH: How does that all start? Where does that happen, in the home? Can any average teen and parent have this turning-the-world-on-its-head kind of approach to life?

MY: Well, all of us can be countercultural. We may not all be funny and wild and crazy and all that kind of stuff. Spontaneity may be difficult for us, but once we begin to think about it — the way you start is to start. Are you willing to take risks and realize that you may fail? Again, one of my key understandings of how we know we live in a pagan culture is not because of drugs and pornography and abortions and sex and alcohol. But it's because we're intimidated. **What Satan does is he intimidates us; he makes us feel we have no value, no worth, and so when we fail, we feel like we've failed.**

But the truth is that failure is a great learning tool. It's a great growth tool, so what is really called for in this day is not really insight and all that. It's courage — the courage to say, "We have to make some changes, and as silly and as awkward as they seem, we've got to do it, or we're not going to make it." I really think that most people are saying: "Show me a plan, give me a book, give me a seminar, give me fourteen things I can do to make a difference in my family." Well, you know, you can do all of that. But ultimately what it takes is courage, the courage to say, "I'm not going to go on like this anymore." You've got to try something new.

Wayne Rice

One thing I've realized is that **parenting is probably the one job, that — once you've learned how to do it — you're done. Once you've acquired the skill of parenting, you're out of a job.**

Once you've acquired the skill of parenting, you're out of a job.

151

Chapter 9

Encouraging Your Child's Spiritual Walk

A classic question that many parents ask is "How can I get my teen to grow closer to God?" What response do you give?

Dennis McCluen

Four things. **Model it.** Kids will not grow unless we are modeling it. Second, **talk about it.** A silent modeling of faith is not simply going to help kids grow as a believer. Testify to what you believe. Third, **integrate it** into life. Get faith worked into the parent's decisions. Ask, "Why do I act the way I do?" Last Sunday it was snowing, and our family was all piling in our car to go to church when we saw a woman stuck in a snowdrift. We talked about how we could rush to church and do the "church thing," while skipping over this woman who needs help. Or, we could assist her. Now if we do, help, we might go to church with mud on us, but that's what faith looks like. So I had a little two minute lecture in the van, then we piled out of the van. We got our shovels and we dug her out. Back in the van, we continued our conversation about why we integrate faith into behavior.

We got our shovels and we dug her out.

So, the fourth way to promote faith in our kids is to **do it together.** Do faith stuff together. Whatever that looks like in your context. Devotions, prayer, worship, study, learning, laughter, intergenerational stuff. Do it together.

Mark Senter

Be consistent with your own walk with God in the home. That's the bottom line. I think when my kids think about spirituality, they're going to remember that I walked with God. Consistency — from my personal habits to my attitude of loving and supporting them. That's essential. **It comes down to you being the person you want them to be.**

For practical examples, I would say "date your kids." I'd say date your spouse as well, but I think there need to be special times that you spend with your kids. Build shared experiences. Take my relationship with my daughter. She is now one of my best friends in the world, but when she was back in high school, I only knew how to relate to boys. I didn't know how to relate

I would say "date your kids."

to girls. About the only thing that I could think of was to take her out to breakfast. And when a girl is 13 years old, eating big breakfasts isn't the best thing in the world for her. And it's funny, I was so nervous. **I'd been in youth work for years, but I was so nervous, especially the first time I dated my daughter, that I actually made out a list of things to talk about! It's true! I asked only the first question, and never got to any of the rest of the list! And as I sat there listening, I realized she wants to be with me.** It was years later, when our son was a sophomore in college; she came down from Canada to watch him play at the University of Dayton. My wife was out of town, so it was just her and me. **We talked until the wee hours of the morning. And one of the things that she said was, "Dad, why didn't we do this earlier?"**

Leith Anderson

This could sound trite, but the best thing that parents can do for their children spiritually is to **live godly lives and live out a good**

marriage. The way we all learn is we look at our models, and we see the way they deal with issues and crises. So, let's just suppose there's a multiple child family, and there's a prodigal child. The parents are primarily focused on how to deal with that prodigal child, but what they're also doing is teaching their children how — and if — they trust in God through one of the most disturbing crises of their life. But that's how they're going to teach their children how to trust God.

I don't think the solution is in family devotions, or that we pray together, or that we all go to church. Those things are important, but the principle in Deuteronomy 6 is *as you go,* you teach your children about God and righteousness. **Often it is the most painful parts of parenting that are the greatest teaching opportunities for what Christianity is all about. It's when you lose your job; it's when you have cancer; it's when you smash up the car. That's when you teach others.** What teenagers need — what we all need — is somebody who is faithful and stable when we are unfaithful and destabilized. What parents need to do is love God and follow Him, not worry a whole lot. Teens see all of that.

> I don't think the solution is in family devotions, or that we pray together, or that we all go to church.

Len Kageler

I have to be vulnerable. I have to share with my kids my own devotions, where I'm struggling, what they can pray for me about. Kids know what's real and they know what's phony. If I'm pretending to be a perfect Christian, they know that nobody's perfect. And if I'm always viewing myself in an authoritarian teacher mode or as the expert — not the "fellow grower in Christ" mode — that's really significant.

Another thing would be: **talk about answers to prayer.** As a family we're praying about things and then celebrating answers to prayer. When our kids were little, we called them "I spy" things,

155

events that could only be explained by the presence of God. Today we don't call them "I spy," we call them miracles, or we just call them answers to prayer. If those kinds of things are part of the family life and the family talk, **there's nobody who can say to this kid: "There is no God." Because they know, beyond a shadow of a doubt, that God lives.** He answers prayer, and He does stuff that only God can do. If the parents are living the Christian life on that level — where they are out on the edge trusting God — and God does respond with powerful answers that can't be denied, that could have a very powerful impact on the home.

Ron Habermas: You said something to begin with that is sort of a paradox. I wonder how intentional it was: the teacher vs. fellow traveler. How intentional is that contrast in your parenting?

LK: The older my kids get, the less I am a teacher and the more I am a fellow traveler. That mode tends to shift that way as our kids grow older. We're very much in the teaching mode when our kids are young children, but when they get into late elementary school, and into adolescence, that line definitely needs to shift into fellow traveler. It's still teaching, but it's not the "I know and you don't" mode.

Haman Cross

I would go back to the whole issue of destiny. **Like Hannah, Samuel's mother, I think that Christian parents need to understand that their child has a spiritual purpose. And we need to know that and say that. Treat them like they were special. Help your teens to hear God's calling.** This kid Samuel matures and leads a special life, even though the spiritual influences in Eli's sons were messed up. But Samuel had a sense of purpose. He had a plan; a destiny. Now, it was not perfect. You can't fully understand it. I was born for a reason, and you can't understand it. I've been used by God and I'm going to run my race, but one thing I've got to do before I leave is that I've got to anoint the next generation.

Help your teens to hear God's calling.

RH: What I find fascinating, with that same analogy, is how Samuel's kid turned out to be like Eli's. Samuel has this professional quality about him, like Eli, and yet both of their domestic fronts had problems.

HC: Actually, when you look at Scripture, it is hard to find two generations of godly people. David blew it! You don't want to think that God is handicapped or something, but He can't do two or three generations in a row!

Mark Cannister

One is simply modeling — that **you can't lead your teen any farther in the faith than you've gone.** Parents need to be modeling a strong Christian faith, a prayer life, the study of Scriptures, significant involvement in the church or in the community. We've got to at least begin with the modeling issue.

It's important for parents to encourage their teenagers to develop their own apologetic of the faith. The way we need to do that is by encouraging teenagers to doubt. Doubting isn't a sin. Disbelief is a sin. One of the problems I see in higher education is students who grew up in great youth groups, came from wonderful Christian families — but when they're finally away from home, they don't have anybody to rely on. All of a sudden, they're starting to ask themselves questions for the first time — "What is it that I really believe?" **Too often we raise kids who just simply accept the beliefs of our church and of our parents. It would be much healthier if, during the high school years, we encourage those kids to doubt their parents' faith a little bit and doubt the church's faith and really investigate what it is that they believe. Help them create ownership of their faith** and not continue to live off the coattails of other people's faith.

Doubting isn't a sin.

Roger Cross

You honor your kid. You honor them by talking to them about the kinds of things you struggle with in your faith. An example of that might be when my boss openly declares that he's homosexual. So as I'm talking to my son, I'm sharing what a tough challenge that is to my faith: I don't believe that's the right lifestyle for my boss, but I also believe that Jesus wanted me to treat this man with compassion. **That brings out real examples in your life, which helps your kids see you're struggling with a real faith.** How does my faith work in this situation?

The other thing that is really incredibly important is to create an environment in your home where questions are acceptable. A kid always has permission to say, "Dad, why?" Let me reemphasize that if a young kid starts asking basic questions, but the environment of that home does not encourage questions, they won't ask the tougher questions as teens either. If they are put down or they don't feel that somebody heard them, they're not going to ask important questions. **One of the greatest revelations in my walk with Christ was that if I can't ask any questions, then God isn't who He says He is. We don't have to be afraid of any questions.**

> If I can't ask any questions, then God isn't who He says He is. We don't have to be afraid of any questions.

Ken Davis

The strongest thing that they can do is to demonstrate how their own personal relationship with God affects their lives. It isn't something you can do. **You can't assign it. And it isn't done by family devotions. Those things are wonderful, but the single greatest thing that parents can do to help their kids grow in their relationship with God is to model that relationship in their own lives.** That way youth get to see their parents grow and change and say, "I'm sorry." They watch their behavior change. They watch them mature. That's the strongest thing that can be done. And I'm not sure that there's much else that works until that's in place.

RH: So it goes back to modeling in those early, early years, those formative years?

KD: I think it does. It extends to the teen years. Kids lives are most impacted when they see something work. Something that can be demonstrated throughout life. It involves a broader aspect of seeing changes in the parents' lives as a result of their walk with God. **Kids ought to see a growing relationship between Mom and Dad as a result. They ought to see a real humility and a lack of misuse of authority as a result. A lack of focus on material things, and a caring for other people. Otherwise — and we've seen this millions of times, even in my own family — you go to church, you go to Sunday School, you have prayer before meals, and you do family devotions. But there's very little foundation — a foundation that'll cause a kid to want to grow. It's just legalism.**

Ginny Olson

Create a safe environment so that the kids, as they work through their faith issues, have a place where they can come home and say, "Guess what? I'm an atheist." And the parent won't freak out, but they can say, "Let's talk about this. Tell me why. Tell me what's going on." **As I talk with college students, they tell me what they appreciated from their parents was, when they were young, they were allowed to question their faith. And the parents are saying, "We still love you even if you don't choose to agree with our belief system."** And that can be very threatening to a parent. What if my kid does not choose God? To let that kid have that freedom. It shows that faith is not something you perform at church on Sundays, but it is part of everyday life.

> Create a safe environment so that the kids . . . have a place where they can come home and say, "Guess what? I'm an atheist."

I remember coming home from college as I was searching through some stuff. My parents and I would be sitting there for two or three hours drinking coffee. And my parents just let me struggle through issues like: "Is it okay to be rich and be a Christian? How do you reconcile that?" Here they are paying my way through college, and I'm asking those kinds of questions. **I loved those times where we could really disagree and yet know that we still cared about each other when we got up from the table.**

Harold Ivan Smith

You start by saying that that job is a parental responsibility which you do not turn over to the youth pastor. I feel that very, very strongly. The youth leader should teach them to pray, teach them to read Scripture, but I do not believe that's being done. He teaches them how to play basketball, but I don't know about their devotional life. What we used to call "family altar" may not be effective, but you need to find time in the day when you're with each child. So I prefer to quote one of David Maines' kids coming home one night and finding his dad stretched out over the couch praying for him. And his father did not know he was home. It was such a powerful influence on him to know that his father prayed for him. **I think a lot of parents pray for their children, but the issue is also praying with your teen, modeling prayer.**

I just did a lecture series on prayer, and I encouraged people at a Christian college to try something. I said, "When you go to lunch today, and somebody prays, I want you to ask them, 'Where did you learn that prayer?' And I want you to see where they learned it." We tend to have prayers for meals very similar to what our parents prayed. They are a bit of a ritual or rote. Sometimes they don't mean a lot, sometimes they do. But it is that sense of praying with our children. Always looking for teachable moments. Interruptible moments. We need to be open, in the power of the Holy Spirit, to be sensitive to those moments. Because what happens, when you don't take advantage of that moment, is that one of your other kids who is listening may say, "Well, I'm certainly not going to talk to Dad about that."

Ask the Holy Spirit to help you be interruptible.

Ask the Holy Spirit to help you be interruptible. I like to use the example of a ball coming over the tennis net, or a ball coming over the volleyball net. Recognize the volley when it comes and participate fully in it. It can be things like leaving some Scriptures on the driver's seat of the car or the windshield, or it could be leaving other little notes. It's reinforcement. **Find creative ways of expressing your love, but also God's love, to that teen. Which also means being open to receiving that love from the teen as well.** Sometimes that means being honest with the teen, saying, "I need you to pray about this; this is a real issue affecting me." Being willing, at times, to be vulnerable with our teens. I wish that some people had the discipline to do it.

Les Parrott

What I recommend to mom and dad (especially those who are very eager and concerned) is that they **steer clear of guilt motivation, when it comes to spiritual issues for their kids.** That's probably the biggest problem that I see of well-intentioned parents, who are trying to get their kids aligned spiritually.

RH: For example, what's a line that parents typically use as a guilt motivator?

LP: Topics on church attendance or about how they treat their sister or brother like: "How do you think God would feel about that?" Anything that's guilt reducing, anything that would try to get those kids to be motivated. **In other words, what you're trying to steer clear of is having them do the right thing for the wrong reasons.** Most moms and dads are concerned about their kids doing the right thing. Yet they do that at all costs. That strategy will backfire on them as soon as those kids get out from underneath their wings.

Steer clear of having them do the right thing for the wrong reasons.

Christian parents should be really concerned, of course, about the whole message of Christ: that we not just do the right thing, but that we do it for the right reasons. We miss that combination sometimes. I know from my own research, that **adolescents carry more guilt — emotional guilt — than any other single age**

group, because they don't measure up to their own expectations for their identity. However, moms and dads often don't see their kids as feeling any kind of guilt, because teens hold it all inside — within tight little packages. They don't reveal any kind of painful emotions.

RH: Do you have a particular resource where you identify that research finding?

LP: Yes, in my book *Love's Unseen Enemy*. There's a chapter near the back on parenting. Then it's also found in my book *Helping the Struggling Adolescent*. **Use of guilt is probably the number one motivational mistake parents make.** We use guilt motivation because it works. The problem is it only works for the short run. **For example, if you want your kid to go to church, or you want your kid to clean up his room, or you want your kid to apologize, guilt motivation will probably work. But it's not going to create a lifestyle of doing good things properly. Actually it will do the very opposite.**

Helen Musick

Start with the parents being honest about their own personal relationship with God. Confess that they're not perfect. I try to say to my young kids, "When it comes to obedience (which is a main issue with my kids), sometimes I struggle with obeying God and being patient with you. I am asking God to help me." Being honest with your kids, at their developmental levels, is important. So, when they are fifteen, hopefully, I'll be able to be vulnerable with them about troubles concerning sexuality or temptation. **My goal is to integrate my kids with — not isolate them from — their world.** To allow them to determine what is right and what is wrong; what is pleasing and what is not, to God. Realize that they have to make choices themselves.

Dave Rahn

I have a strong opinion about this. It's simple, yet not simplistic. The single best thing I can do is to invigorate my own rela-

tionship with God. Out of that vitality, I continue to work on a healthy relationship with my teens. **If I've got a great love relationship with my teen and he or she knows that I love my Lord, that's the best thing that I can do to help him.** I want parents to think about the reality that, sometimes, teens — for their own health and development — have to test things out themselves. They have to own it. And I have to give them room to own it. That's another reason that modeling, as a strategy, is not intrusive. It's attractive.

RH: Tell me how you get intimate with God and have it show?

DR: Sometimes you think that you have to have your devotions in a pretty conspicuous place.

RH: Like right in front of the TV.

DR: Yeah, like "You guys can watch TV if you want, just let me pray." But, seriously, I really think it's about living your life very fully for Christ. Living very openly about what you do and why you do it. To the degree that it's possible to involve them — come along, tag along — that's fine. But I want my kids to understand that the reason I'm involved as a volunteer with Campus Life is not because I love other kids, taking time away from our family. I want them to understand it's about this non-Christian kid coming to know Christ. **So, I involve them and ask them: "Can you help me pray for them?" To bring my kids in on the strategy. That's been a fun element to me. That'll begin to work itself into their world, by me simply asking questions like "Who are some of your friends?" Just asking basic questions: "Anything I can do to help?"** "Do you think your friends would like to go on a campout, where we just kind of hang out?" Maybe one night I get a chance to share some verses with everybody. Always really respecting their role with their friends. I think it becomes increasingly important, with teenagers, for me to be as openly reflective about what's going on — why I do what I do in my walk with the Lord — as I can.

RH: I hear you saying a few things here that have connectedness. You're transparent in front of your kids, in terms of your own day-to-day passions and objectives. You bring them in, by letting them peek over your shoulder. And then you say, to yourself, "Because I've shown you part of my world, let me look into yours. Here're a couple of things; what do you think about them?"

DR: And periodically, I ask for some feedback about how I'm doing in light of their expectations. Here's a very concrete example: My boy is a basketball and baseball player. Pretty competitive; pretty good. One of the things that has irritated me is how animated he can be, when calls don't go his way. We've just about talked this topic to death, it seems like. After a ball game last week, we got on that issue again. Very quickly. He had a good game; he did very well. Yet we quickly focused on this perpetual challenge: his facial expressions, his scowling, things like that. That set the tone. And talking about it made it a bummer for him and me. So I said, "Jason, I don't want to do this. I don't want to make you feel bad. I want to enjoy the positive. But I just get aggravated with your face — not your play — your attitude. And maybe it's because I'm there. Maybe the best thing would be for me to just stay away. I don't know." Then I said, "We need to talk some more, but I don't want to talk at you. So when you want to talk more, come on down from your room." About a half an hour later, he came down and said, "Let's kick this around. Let's talk about it." I said, "Just tell me what you want from me. What would be good, for you, from me?" He said he wanted a lot of involvement from me. For instance, I love talking to him about every single play he made in the game. Well, he wants that. He loves talking about it with me. Sometimes I feel like I'm hyperanalytical. Well, he likes that. And yet he still wants me to remind him about this face. So we now have a gesture that we worked out. He likes that. **I said, "Ok, I'm glad to know that. Now, here's my criteria: 'Try your best to respect other people and enjoy yourself.' That's all I care about."** It was a really good conversation. His next game was his best effort and productivity. And his best face that I've ever seen him have! **And it all happened because I asked him to tell me what he wanted from me. That's a good relationship measuring stick, I think.**

RH: I hear you challenging the world's perspective of sports and competition. I hear you saying, "We're not going to drop out of the world's system by pulling you off the team. We're going to change the system itself by making you a different person on the team."

DR: Exactly. I want to keep talking about that to him. If he always knows "here's what's important to Dad" then, eventually, I hope it kicks in for him. I've tried to figure out how I might have added to his struggles. Maybe I'm just talking to him too much to make the whole thing too important.

RH: How do you live fully for Christ in front of teens?

DR: To live fully for Christ, in front of teens, can't be contrived. It has to be very natural. I have to live fully for Christ because that's the way Christ wants it. There needs to be a visible side that processes things out loud, that talks about how much TV we'll watch, what kind of TV we'll watch, our friends, how we talk about other people, how we pray, how we enjoy each other. And as important as anything: owning up to my mistakes, asking their forgiveness, or letting them see me ask forgiveness of my wife when I make mistakes. Otherwise, the experience in the home can come across as too demanding, or it can look like we're seeking perfection.

David Olshine

To be honest, I don't. I don't help parents do that. **Ultimately, I can't help parents help their kids love Jesus. They have to do it.** They have to model it. They have to be passionate. **Vince Lombardi once said that fatigue makes cowards of us all, or something like that. I think we've got a generation of fatigued parents who, when they get home, are spiritually empty. Spiritual cowards, perhaps.** So, I think the name of the game is passion and priorities. Sounds like a

> We've got a generation of fatigued parents who, when they get home, are spiritually empty. Spiritual cowards, perhaps.

165

good title of a book, doesn't it? Passion and priorities. I think the kids see it. It's modeling. I personally can't do anything for a parent to help them grow. I can give them some perspective, but the only thing I can do is for my wife Rhonda and my daughter Rachel and me. I really don't know that I can equip anyone else to pull that off.

Jay Kesler

You don't talk about love, you love. You don't talk about forgiveness, you forgive. You don't talk about patience, you're patient. Jesus just walked through life with His disciples. I think parents must be walking with their kids through life, being very conscious that the Lord is an ever present help in time of need. Teaching all the time. All moments are teaching moments.

So, you're watching something on TV and something strange is said. You stop and say, "How does that relate to what we believe? What would happen if our family started practicing this behavior?" and so on. **We constantly challenge the culture, in light of our biblical presuppositions, and make them teaching moments. Because an awful lot of undigested junk is coming to kids through media. Just crazy stuff. Someone needs to stop and say, "Now wait a minute! Do we really believe this? What would happen if someone really did this?" Suddenly it dawns on you —
this is make-believe. This wouldn't work in real life. This is all part of Christian education and growth in Christ.**

Seeing a parent practicing the presence of God is most convincing instruction with kids, though youngsters might not call it that. But, later they tend to talk to their friends about it, like: "My dad is consistent. My mom does this all the time."

Marlene LeFever

First of all, I suppose, is to make sure you really love Him. Some days, if teens love Jesus the way I do, there wouldn't be much hope for Christianity. We all go through times like that. **I'm not convinced that dry periods are bad. Parents can help their youth grow in personal relationships with God by showing their**

own growth patterns. So, if they're involved in a Bible study and get really excited about what they learned and share that in a non-didactic way, this tells the teen **it's okay to stay excited about Jesus.** We want to continue growing during our adult years, and that's what children need to see. If they see that example, then that becomes a really exciting model.

Another strategy is stressing commitment to real service. I was in Minneapolis the other day, at a large church, and they have an acre or so of land that is dedicated to doing gardens in the summertime. **The teenagers help with this work, and their job is to create the best garden they could possibly create. All the food goes to the homeless. Teens are expected to keep these in good shape.** Also, several of them were going through confirmation classes. And it's a nice balance — this passage into church life at a semiadult level. They're expected to do something like this. I like that. They're setting real service goals in front of them. If you're going to be confirmed in this church, you've got to have a service that makes sense. And cleaning up the church nursery or picking up trash in the front yard is not enough. Neither is going on a mission trip where you have fun for five days. **Some people will get their hands dirty by working with their *minds*, and that's fine. But let's see what Christianity's *legs* look like.**

It's okay to stay excited about Jesus.

Dan Bautista

Parents must lead by example. My oldest daughter has been doing personal devotions by herself for the last year and a half or so. Last summer, one of our camp counselors asked me, "What did you do to get your daughter to do devotions?" But I didn't even know how it happened. My wife and I never told her she had to do them. We never even hinted about it. There's no magic formula. It just happened. There has been a turning point in her own spiritual growth. God's been speaking to her alone, and using the Word of God to speak to her heart. I said to her, "Over the summer somebody asked

167

me about your devotions. I told them that I'm glad you're doing it. But what motivated you?" She said, "I don't know. I think it's important, and every Christian should do it." She does her devotions like her mother does. Maybe that's what happened. If there's one thing that could help teens, it's personal example. **If parents are going to do personal devotions, it should be something natural. If they're going to go to church, enjoy it. It should be something natural. Teens should know their parents are doing something because they enjoy it. Because it's part of them.**

Wayne Rice

Unless we, as parents, are also growing in our own personal relationship with God — and we model that in front of kids — then our own kids are not going to grow either. **I don't have to preach at my kids very much, because they know what makes me tick. They see the kinds of books that are always sitting next to my chair. They see all the things that my wife Marcie and I are involved in. They watch and they see — this is how it's done. This is how you grow in your relationship with God.** It's not something you just mail in. It takes effort; it takes work; it means getting up in the morning and sometimes staying out late. It means making sacrifices.

I have a friend, who (like me) likes to fish. He goes fishing on Sunday morning, and I told him, "You're a fool." (He's a good friend of mine, and I can say that to him.) He's got two kids watching him, so what he's teaching them is this: "You don't need to go to church to grow in your relationship with God." But, **one nonnegotiable in our family is that we're there in church on Sundays. Unless we're all on our death bed, we're there.** It's just modeling, and that's how it sinks in.

You can't preach at your kids. I think you can talk about these things. I think you should involve them in your conversations when you're having discussions about faith issues — what you're struggling with. As I've gotten older, I personally have taken on more of that quiet time. You know, solitude. When I was younger, the way I grew in my relationship with God was to work for Him. I think kids also need to have an opportunity for service. They may not know how to get close to God any other way than just to serve Him. Getting involved in ministry and missions. They get close to God that way, and later they will discover the need just to cuddle up and spend time in the Word.

Rick Dunn

Model your own spiritual life. Make it a natural part of your life. Like Deuteronomy 6. More spirituality is going to be caught than taught. Help teens find mentors and peers, because the older they get, the less parents are to be the only resource they have. **So don't be intimidated by the fact that your fourteen year old needs some other adult in their life.**

Also, I'm not one for gearing our approach, as parents, with teenagers' spiritual lives toward much content. There is a time to give that, but the content arrives in discussions that take place in meaningful experiences like camping, teaching a Sunday school class, going on a mission trip, or helping at a soup kitchen. **Being active together is when teachable moments come.** Otherwise, I think you are missing the point of adolescent spirituality, from a parent's perspective.

Thom Schultz

It goes back to long term vision again. That is, keep priorities straight. **We need to be very careful that, as parents, we are sending signals that say — in a lot of different ways — "a relationship with God is the top priority."** When it comes to family schedule (and the schedule of everything else that encroaches on our time), do we send out the signals that are consistent, saying that our relationship with God is the top priority? The church can help here with how it schedules programs. **Sometimes the best "program" we can do is to downsize our programs at church to allow families to concentrate on what is really important.**

RH: Once you have this long term vision and your priorities straight, how does that move into the teen's lives? How do I, as a parent, help them with their own growth?

TS: I think parents often forget the power of the eavesdropper. Kids are picking up a lot more by what they eavesdrop from their parents than from what we may be deliberately lecturing. We could concentrate a little bit less on lecturing and try to guide kids more by how we are modeling the faith, what we are saying, and allowing kids to overhear us. To watch us.

The respect and the love that I have for the Bible today is based on nothing that my parents ever said. It's based on the many, many times when I came home from school or from an activity and caught my dad sitting in his chair with his Bible. He usually never even related to me what he was reading that day. Nor did he choose that opportunity to give me a little minisermon. He allowed me to eavesdrop on how important God was in his life. Our kids are so in tune with what we're doing, even though we may not fully sense that. The more opportunities we simply allow them to eavesdrop on in our lives — where they hear us talking about how faith is a live part of what we're doing, when they see us face problems and adversity — that's so much more powerful than any lecture or minisermon or any family devotion time that we could plan.

> Parents often forget the power of the eavesdropper ... my father allowed me to eavesdrop on how important God was in his life.

Mike Yaconelli

Well, I'm 54. **It took me until I was 50 to know what intimacy with God even meant. I had, quite frankly, never experienced it.** I could talk about Jesus. I could tell people all about Him. I could introduce people to Jesus, which I did. I knew everything there was to know about Jesus, but I did not genuinely have an intimate relationship with Jesus. **I'm convinced that where most of us flounder is that we think we need to get our kids to understand Christianity, to recognize that it's true, and to act on that recognition. Really what we need to do is to be intimate with Jesus ourselves, so that when our kids are around us, they see us in the presence of God, in the presence of Jesus, living as though Jesus were there, living in that kind of intimacy. That passion for God will do more than anything else I can think of.**

RH: I hear you partially contrasting the cognitive, more traditionalist perspective with a more affective, experiential one. Is that a fair assessment?

MY: Yeah. I mean, I'm all for thinking and engaging our minds in what the gospel is about. **But ultimately what kids remember are not the talks and the logic. They remember that experience they had with God, or that relationship.** If I say to my own kids, "What do you love most about our church? Is it the way I'm a really cool speaker, and my really neat talks that I give on Sunday morning?" Nah. They'd say, "Stu Higgs." Married 40 years. Wife leaves him. He gets MS. He's struggling along; he's slowly becoming weaker and weaker. He loves my kids. He calls them and talks to them. That's what they remember. We need to recognize that, through the relationship that we have with Jesus, these kids will notice those human relationships.

RH: So, it's the relationships that you help them get attached to?

MY: You don't need to help them. All they need to see is what's going on in your life. I don't need to point it out to them. If they ask me, obviously, I'm going to tell them. There will be times when I will talk about my faith because, at that moment, my faith is integrated with the life experience. I can't talk about it without talking about my faith. But, it's not an artificial educational model where I sit them down and make sure they understand what we believe and why, and then get them to sign a doctrine of faith.

Chapter 10
Stepping Back Into Time

If you could enter H.G. Wells' time machine, what event or person would you want to revisit — perhaps even take teens and their parents with you — in order to help them in the 21st century?

Haman Cross

I'd like to talk to Mary, Jesus' mother, when she gets pregnant before she gets married, and ask her: "What was that like? How did you deal with that?" I see in Scripture every example of what we face, as parents of teenagers. Issues regarding children, and blended families, extended families and different cultures. How did they do it? What worked and what didn't work?

> I'd like to talk to Mary, Jesus' mother, when she gets pregnant before marriage and ask her: "What was that like? How did you deal with that?"

Leith Anderson

I'd like to be there when Jonathan Edwards was fired from his church in Northfield, and when he moved to Princeton. The story is detailed in Elizabeth Dodd's book *Marriage to a Difficult Man*. Jonathan Edwards, I think, had seven children. He was God's agent in the Great Awakening. His church voted him out. He then moved his wife and children to a ministry where they lived out in the forest, ministering to Native Americans. He moved from there to become the president of Princeton University. At the end of Dodd's book is a well known study that traces their family and compares it to another family. That other family produced only people who lived on the public dole and in jail for generations of about 200 years. **Jonathan Edwards' family produced a vice-president of the United States, senators, physicians, and ministers. It's just amazing. But they did it out of hardship and difficulty. The way they dealt with those tough issues enormously impacted their children, in a way that was then spread out for generations to come.** It'd be a great story to be able to look back and say — and to see — how did they do that? How did they deal with this troublesome point so triumphantly?

Ron Habermas: Which gets back to your previous point about crises.

LA: Yes, it's usually the worst times that turn out to be the best times.

I don't think that you can teach someone how to behave in a crisis.

RH: Are there any principles here that you see to be valuable, Leith? Besides the obvious matter of being faithful, what else makes such success stories, according to your experience? How do you pass that kind of faith on?

LA: I don't think it's contrived. I think that people who have faith and trust God, that is the way they behave in crises. I don't think that you can teach someone how to behave in a crisis. We've all done this: you sit down with somebody and say, "What was the time when you were closest to God?" Everybody, without exception, says the worst times. Nobody ever says when I won the lottery or won the gold medal at the Olympics. It's always in difficulty. So what we need to do is say that you trust God with all your heart. You most discover what that means when you go through the most difficult times. **That is why the worst times are the best times. That is very encouraging.**

Harold Ivan Smith

I pick the time when Clyde Narramore came to Pasadena College around 1960. I'm not sure about the exact year. It was just a chance to deliver a little chapel talk. There was a young man sitting in that audience who came from a generation of preachers, and he thought that he was also supposed to be a preacher, since far back on one side of his ancestry, everyone had been preachers. Yet he didn't feel called to be a preacher. It was just the pressure. But after an incredible chapel, that young man asked to meet the speaker and he ended up getting an appointment. Dr. Narramore was very gracious to him, and said, "Well, here are some of the options you could have," including Christian counseling. That was the turning point for a young tennis player named James Dobson, and all the world has been changed because of that.

There are a couple of factors here: first, that somebody encouraged him to go make an appointment with Dr. Narramore and talk to him. Second, that Dr. Narramore had even been willing to accept that chapel; what if someone else had spoken in chapel that day instead of Clyde Narramore? Finally, what I've also seen is that it was a freeing moment for James Dobson, because he realized that God wasn't calling him to preach, but that God was calling him into another kind of ministry. That is one of the crucial events of this century, yet I'm sure it doesn't seem that way to many. But look at the impact of Focus on the Family and the lives that they've touched.

I think about that when I speak in chapel: who is the one person that I'm talking to that could make a difference? Or that appointment, that hot dog or hamburger meeting? Turning points. Where you later look back and see that was a turning point. What if Narramore had been too busy for this young Dobson, or what if he had said, "You've got two minutes, that's all the time I'm going to give you." **It really is kind of scary, when you think about all**

these chance encounters (that seem to be chance to us), that are part of God's good timing. It makes us pay more attention.

Mike Yaconelli

I'd love to be back when Jesus lived. I'd love to hang around Him and follow Him. I really think that that's all we do anyway as good ministers, parents, and teachers; we continually look at the life of Jesus.

RH: Give me one day that would be helpful to set the time machine for, one event in Jesus' life that you wish you could see first hand, or help parents of teens see.

MY: The day that Jesus was crucified, in order to experience the loss, the crumbling of my hopes and expectations, and the incredible loneliness and despair and bitterness. Then to recognize that God is bigger than that. That would be critical. I think that that is something lacking in all of our lives. **We want everything fixed; we want answers.** So, to experience the disintegration of what I now believe, so that I can believe something that is new and bigger is what's difficult, yet important.

Thom Schultz

The date I'd pick is today. I'd put today on hold. That would give me the unique opportunity to put all the short-term busyness aside, and to concentrate for as long as I wanted to on what's most important for our family today. The fantasy of that possibility intrigues me, and sets my imagination rolling in terms of how things would different, if I had that opportunity. Yet, in reality, we all have that chance every day. If I really want to, I can put a lot of stuff that is cluttering our life as a family on hold, and take a look at the top priorities and the long-term vision in a whole new way.

RH: So, for you, this time-travel analogy should guard us against busyness that's unwarranted, but also against low priorities that jump up to the top of our lives?

TS: Yes, all the distractions.

Len Kageler

I'd love to see a historic catastrophe that would show them how good we have it today. It would put into perspective the little problems that we often complain about. I would like them to see that, when they're living in a village and the cart is going down their street every day for people to bring out their dead. That really tends to make other problems less important. **If our kids could just understand how good we have it.**

Wayne Rice

On a personal note, something that is in my own memory banks, I'd like to revisit a series of events from my own childhood with my father. **One of my favorite memories of my dad is that he always laughed at my jokes. And I'll always be grateful for that, grateful for his wisdom. Because I've listened to my** own kids' jokes, and they're pretty terrible — and I have a feeling that mine were too. In fact, I know they were. But my dad honored me by laughing at my jokes.

One of my favorite memories of my dad is that he always laughed at my jokes.

Mark Senter

I would have loved to have gone to Portland, Maine, and sat in the first Christian Endeavor Group, and see the kids respond — committing themselves to know God. There was holiness in that movement.

Even more than that, I would have loved to have experienced, with some kids, Paxton on his horse in the Midwest, starting Sunday Schools. I would like to have gone along to see the way Sunday School missionaries — most of whom were very young people — had a profound impact upon towns. They started Sunday Schools during the Great Valley Campaign in about 1832-1834. The influence of those people was great — reshaping the society, the impact upon even alcohol consumption, starting libraries, and starting churches.

These were all young people that were doing ministry. Passionate young missionaries. It would be great to take some kids along to be part of this movement. Just a two-year period where God was doing some incredible stuff. About 5000 churches were established as a result of these Sunday Schools. **One of the ways we're going to shape this generation is by setting them free on missions of different sorts.**

Rick Dunn

To be present during Jesus' conversation with Mary and Joseph, after He stayed at the temple — that would be an intriguing experience to see an adolescent who was making some differentiations, while not sinning. **One of the challenges for parents today is to discern between differentiation and rebellion.** Particularly because it is such a lengthy part of the parent-teen experience.

RH: Describe that further: "Differentiation that is not rebellion."

RD: My son wants to get his ear pierced. Some parents immediately think that is rebellion; it is not Christian. It may not have anything to do with that. Or, your kid wants to go hear some music that you are not quite sure of. He wants to go to a concert that you think is real trash. It's often tempting to jump at it like: "Why would you want to listen to something that is not very Christian?" It might be that they are trying to sort out (or try out) their friends. It is also possible that they *are* in rebellion. That can incline them towards some trashy stuff, but I don't know that just from a decision to go to a concert. It takes some time to discern that.

The other response I thought of was not a time factor, but a cultural factor. **I'd like to go to those cultures that have rites of passage.** See some of the ways those issues are worked out. Maybe some tribal countries. Not that I am going to follow their custom, but to understand how their customs work in terms of their kids' progress from child to adulthood. American culture has only a couple of rites of passage, like going from junior high to senior high or getting a driver's license. But there is really not anything that can help you identify "I'm a child," "I'm an adolescent," and "I'm an adult." All the lines are blurred. I had a friend in my doctoral program who was from Rwanda, in a very, very poor part of Africa. But, in the evening there, the old men in the village got all the children around a fire and told them stories. Life stories. I got this picture of them sitting around, the old men teaching the young children. And I thought: **"These men are telling life stories in Africa on the same night where kids in America are sitting around watching Nickelodeon." Which culture is really nourishing kids?** So I would like to interact with those cultures.

The idea of a village raising the kid is a strong concept. It's unfortunate that some Christians will not use that truth, because Hillary Clinton wrote on that theme. But it's a wonderful way to think about families.

Dave Rahn

That's a fun question. I'd choose Joseph in the Bible. I'd like to have a conversation with Joseph, late in his life. I'd like Joseph to talk about the dynamics of his family — why he thought certain things happened. I'd like Joseph to spin his story of being cast out by his brothers and ending up in exile. I'd probe him. **I expect Joseph didn't hold grudges. He would continue to talk about God's role, God's sovereignty, God's design, and how it all worked out for good. But, I would say, "Did you know that at the time it was all happening? How did you cope with it, at the time?"**

My goal would be to widen the perspective, to reinforce this very hopeful concept that God knows what He is doing. That today's momentary troubles don't dictate the course of an entire life. It's the way you respond to those troubles, challenges, and opportunities. Joseph is a great example of that. We generally live in a culture that's weaker in character, because we tend to think that it's the things happening to us which make life good. And Joseph didn't wait for that. That's not what defined his life.

RH: So, let me get this quotable quote from you: "It's not the troubles in life that we should focus on, but how we respond to the troubles." Is that what you're saying?

DR: Yes, absolutely.

RH: I also hear you saying that, the world tells us to do just the opposite: "Put all the fires out."

DR: The world defines my quality of life by the things that come to me. But I believe that quality of life is how I embrace whatever comes to me. There's a huge difference. My favorite little parable, in this direction, is about a surfer. If you can imagine a beach scene where you've got two different settings. One setting is a family with a little child who's wandering in and out of the surf. Finally a big wave cuts loose, knocks the kid down, and he comes up crying with a big fat lip sticking out. So he doesn't want anything to do with the ocean. But in the second setting, at the very same beach, there's this surfer with a twinkle in his eye. That same wave is just what he wants. There's no difference in the wave. The difference is in their ability to handle the wave and how to approach it. **One time you might say, "I don't want that wave. It's a bad wave. That ruins my life." Another time you say, "Bring it on! The bigger the better! It's a great challenge!"**

RH: Realizing it's dangerous, too.

DR: It is dangerous. But in the danger I learn, I grow. And you get up from the experience — kind of shaken — and say, "That was a tough one. I hope I'm ready for the next time." It's a very different approach to life and faith. It's like the approach that Paul had when he experienced his incredible joy in jail, as he writes to the believers at Philippi. Just a huge difference in perspective.

Roger Cross

I'd like to take families back to a time where Christian families were living in a difficult culture. Where they were really struggling. For instance, go back and live with a Christian family in Germany during the height of the Hitler regime. Or go back to when the Early Church persecution started. I'd like for current families to see how those families handled troublesome situations. **First, I hope they'd see how a family can pull together in a crisis. Second, how their faith in God helped them in these situations.**

Ginny Olson

What popped into my mind was to take a family back to when the parents were kids. To remind parents that they were not perfect. That they struggled with some of the things their kid struggles with, but also to find that culture has changed drastically. Some things have stayed the same, but some things are very, very different. And for kids to get a new perspective, like: "Wow, my parents have not always been thirty-something or forty-something. They are real people." To get a little bit of a bigger perspective. There's some humanness here.

> What popped into my mind was to take a family back to when the parents were kids. To remind parents that they were not perfect.

Marlene LeFever

I'd like to spend about two or three days with Abraham and Sarah in their tents, because we think that our modern family structure is so fragmented and so alone. I'd like kids today to see that Ishmael didn't have a father in the traditional sense. That the entire village raised the kids, not just one woman. I'd like them to see a sense of pride in my clan, my group's tents, rather than just my own home. I'd like them to see that community. And it would be isolated out there in the desert. It would be more pure than what we see now. And, maybe by sticking it in a different geographical setting, **kids would come to realize how important it is to be a part of a church family.**

> I'd like kids today to see that Ishmael didn't have a father in the traditional sense.

181

Mark Cannister

Go back to an agrarian society for maybe a week. Maybe back to Walton's Mountain! Where the whole family was really a whole family. Experience that for a while, and then try to think through how we translate that setting into our modern society. There may be some aspects of technology we have now that we're not taking full advantage of. We might actually be able to be closer to each other (even though we live thousands of miles apart) by using the technology that we have available to us. Recapture some of the closeness the agrarian society seemed to have: growing up on the farm, doing chores, communicating around the dinner table, and so forth. Maybe that's too romantic a view of the agrarian society, but I think I'd like to look back at that a little bit.

Jay Kesler

The worst example I've ever read was Thomas Jefferson's relationship with his kids. He actually wrote them letters and said, "If you don't perform well in this area, your father won't love you." He literally tried to withhold his love.

The other negative one is young Winston Churchill. Here's this little kid who's living in a boarding school; his mother is in the newspapers as a socialite, a plaything as it were; his dad is involved in the Parliament and very busy. His dad's in meetings right across the street from the school and doesn't visit the boy for about a year at a time. Here is this little, fat, lonely boy being picked on by everybody — not too bright and smart. The fact that this kid turned out to be anything is amazing to me, because **no parents ever did more wrong things toward a child then they did toward Winston Churchill. And yet, somehow, it once again gives me faith in the basic stuff that people are made of. That there is the grace of God. People can recover, sometimes, from terrible kinds of neglect. To me this is beautiful.**

RH: Maybe seeing a negative example might help them appreciate all the more what they have.

JK: Frankly, I think most of the examples are negative — they're stories of the overcomers. I think one of the problems in this culture is that we've made victimization an industry. People think that the world's supposed to be fair. The former generation didn't think the world was fair. It wasn't fair; it was terribly unjust, and people overcame difficulties. One thing I think that's important to kids and adults is the realization that literature has changed so dramatically. We don't have any more of the Horatio Alger kinds of stories, the overcomers.

> We've made victimization an industry. People think that the world's supposed to be fair. The former generation didn't think the world was fair. It wasn't fair; it was terribly unjust, and people overcame difficulties.

Down at the lake I have a Jack London short story book. I was reading these old short story books that I used to read as a kid. I gave them to my grandson to read. They're all stories of courage; stories of heroics. In today's world you have all these stories of the world coming unglued, ever since Hemingway and Steinbeck began to deal with the exposure of the psychological nature of culture. All the books are about psychology now, not about real people and their real heroics. Kids need to read these heroic stories. **These are extremely important to put in front of them: heroic stories from history. It's a terrible shame that most kids don't know much about the great heroes.**

Helen Musick

The person that I would talk to was Sherlock Holmes, because he had the ability to figure out problems. I wish I could talk to him about unlocking some of the mysteries of parenting in the culture that we're in.

David Olshine

In I Chronicles 13:9, when the Israelites came to the threshing floor of Tedon, Uzzah reached out his hand to steady the Ark of the Covenant because the ox stumbled. The Lord's anger burned against Uzzah, and He struck him down because he had put his hand on the Ark of the Covenant. He died there before God. If I had been him, I might have done the same thing. The ox is stumbling; you see the Ark possibly falling; you'd want to help. **I'd like to take my teens back to that Scripture. I'd like to get in the H.G. Wells' time machine and head back to I Chronicles 13. Watch it, witness it, and talk about that event with my kids.**

That's going to bring about two things that we'd talk about. First, would we have done the same thing? We might get to the question of what's "hands off" for a teenager. What should they not be doing, not be touching. I'm going to be asking the same thing (as a parent) in my relationship with them: What should I not be doing *for* them; figuratively, what should I not be touching? There's a time to "touch" with a kid, as far as *getting involved* with them, and there's a time to *let go.* **Second, that experience from I Chronicles would also strike the fear of God in them. It would cause them to think through doing things that upset parents and know how to draw the lines of restraint.** You know, each teen is going to internalize and say, "Wow, I've done some stuff to my parents that's probably worthy of God killing me. I've said some things to my parents that God should have knocked me dead for."

Chapter 11
Hope for Blended Families

Are there any strategies that you suggest for the blended families in our churches and culture today?

Rick Dunn

Don't watch "The Brady Bunch"! That's a waste of experience concerning what a blended family is like. Communicate that it's okay *not* to try to be the ideal family. I think that everyone is trying to work too hard, so that this perfect family will workout. There is not enough attention given for the unique relationships that the father has with his kids and the mother has with her kids. Many parents find themselves trying so hard to overcompensate and make sure that the other kid's don't feel left out. But, in truth, you wind up creating competition between the kids. Different personalities are going to act differently.

> Don't watch "The Brady Bunch"!

Mark Cannister

There's this commercial from the guy that plays Niles on "Frasier." He's talking about families. He's talking about families communicating. Then he gives a suggestion about how they can communicate better. **As he steps to the side of the screen, he unveils the dinnertable, with the punchline, "Get your family around this thing at least once a week."** When I saw that, I just thought, "Wow, what a sad commentary that the advice we're giving families is to at least get around the table once a week. Could we perhaps shoot a little higher than that? Could our goal be stretched just a little bit?" I'm thinking, "Boy, if secular society is thinking that it would be a great improvement to get people around the table once a week, then we really have a long way to go." **Mealtimes need to have major importance.** But the blended family — more than anybody — needs to probably really have those family times together. That may take the form of family vacation. That may take the form of family meetings or whatever. But focus on family time, one way or another.

> Mealtimes need to have major importance.

Leith Anderson

In history, blended families were the norm, not the exception. Yet we've gone through a fifty year period where they were the exception rather than the norm. Because of precedents with mortality in childbirth and dangers of daily life, blended families were very, very common. So we're really returning, for a different reason, to something — historically and biblically — that was always there. **Jesus was part of a blended family.** The advice, I think, is that there are specific issues that they've got to deal with.

Ron Habermas: What kinds of issues would be helpful for them to know about?

> Jesus was part of a blended family.

LA: Number one, it's very difficult. Number two, unless the children are very young when the families are blended, the children are going to clearly identify with the original parent in a way that they will never identify with the added parent. **Parents need to understand what their own family of origin issues are and how that impacts those particular, blended children. Joint custody issues have significant reli-**

gious impact. For example, what we face for grade school children at our church is that they're often in church on different weekends. So blended family parents are dealing with relationships that are outside of their control, which most two-parent homes don't have.

Wayne Rice

I say this with some fear and trembling because I've never been a part of a blended family. I've only known people who are in them. Secondly, I'm not a family therapist. So for what it's worth, I would just say to parents of blended families: **Don't force your kids to accept a role that's uncomfortable for them. Kids often rebel because they're forced to love their new parents, to treat them like their natural mother or father.** It takes time to build relationships with your new kids and your new family.

Les Parrott

In blended families, we need to recognize that all members have lost an important primary relationship. We need to help them understand grief, and not to bury that grief. We also need to recognize that the relationship between a parent and his or her kids predates the relationship with their new partner. That certainly has some ramifications. A new stepparent is probably going to have to compete with the kids for their actual parent's attention to some degree. Because of that, some stepparents feel that their roles are ill-defined.

Harold Ivan Smith

Blended families, that's tough. I remember going to hear John and Emily Fisher, who were a blended family themselves with nine or ten children. He's a psychiatrist. She's a psychologist. It was a sobering meeting because John did about a

They said: "Either you help us tonight, or we're going to see the lawyer in the morning."

45 minute presentation, and then he opened it up to questions. And I never will forget that there was a man who stood up and said, **"Either you help us tonight, or we're going to see the lawyer in the morning to get a divorce. We can't all of us live together."**

The thing that troubles me is that so many of the blended family issues don't even begin to be dealt with until after there is a marriage. You are trying to sort out, especially with teenagers, their sexuality, and sometimes the parent's sexuality. There is bonding going on. All of those changes. There are some pieces of advice I give: First you need plenty of time, and you need plenty of support. You're going to have to find, in your community, places of support. The sad thing is, in this culture, you can go back across the years, throughout this culture, and find the sad stories of blended families. You had an incredible number of children, even as late as the 1930's and 1940's who fended for themselves, or were put out of their homes, because of the power of the blended family. It's sort of the Cinderella story. That's a strong theme in our culture. Like an iceberg, it's not the 10% above the waterline that you see that sinks the ship, but the 90% below. That's what I tell blended families. On the surface, this may look wonderful, but beneath the surface there are some real issues.

There is a wonderful cartoon inside the *Phi Delta Kappa* this month: There's this little boy pictured with an assignment in art class to draw a picture of his parents. So the student says to the art teacher, "If we don't have enough room for all of the parents on the front side, can we use the back?" And you know, the people I have shown that cartoon to have said, "That's exactly right." Like my chaplain supervisor at the hospital and the therapist. And along with the blending is — and we're seeing this in our cultural rituals — how do you do funerals? With all these people, now, are they step-grandparents, step-great-grandparents?

Roger Cross

I would have somewhat the same advice for the blended family that I would have for the single family. The blended family needs outside sources to help with the healing and growth process. **When you try to blend families, you've got some great obstacles, and I think you need a counselor or somebody that can help you on a regular basis.**

RH: Can parents financially afford that on a regular basis?

RC: I think they've got to find a way. Or to find somebody in the church that has that counseling gift. I don't necessarily think that their help has to be a professional, although that can be helpful. **They need some godly wisdom.**

Dan Bautista

You need to be open with teenagers about mistakes, perhaps why the first or second marriage didn't work, and what makes this current marriage different from the others. Then, be consistent with both sets of kids, especially with teenagers. My fourteen year old tends to be a little more legalistic about things like fairness and justice. She tends to be very ideal. **When you have a blended marriage, you have to give teens the background like you would in a crime scene: this is what happened, this is the result, here we are, and this is what we're going to live with. I think something that frustrates teenagers a lot is not being consistent with how you treat them.**

> When you have a blended marriage, you have to communicate to teens the background, like you would in a crime scene.

Thom Schultz

I've found it really useful to set a rule of no put-downs. Put-downs are off limits. That's an especially healthy rule in a blended family. When you're dealing with all those new relationships, all the people in that house need to live under that rule: put-downs are not allowed. It's also off limits to put down people outside of that house, particularly the absent parents. **The first rule is no** put-downs for those inside the blended family, and the second rule pertains to no put-downs for the other set of parents who are not living there.

Len Kageler

My highest recommendation would be to get involved in a missions trip or a service project together. When you're doing things for other people, it gets your focus off you and your relationships. **Establish a common task.** There is nothing more unifying than that. I've seen a lot of blended families succeed, and not a few fail. The ones who have succeeded are the ones who have, from time to time, celebrated, "Hey, we're accomplishing something together. We're doing something for other people." **The way we are wired, as humans, shows us there is something special that happens in our lives, when we see gratitude on the face of someone else, because of what we've done for them.**

We're not a blended family. But when we moved to the East Coast, the second Christmas we were here, we were still hurting over the fact that we had left people. **We went into Harlem on Christmas morning, and we worked in a soup kitchen. That was bonding for us.** You can see the gratitude on people's faces. Consequently, you don't have to go on a distant missions trip, in order to see many areas where you can serve as a family. Look for projects that help families be unified.

RH: Someone should come along with challenging, missions group projects for blended families. A special mission's focus just for them. This agency could also help them debrief their experiences. It could be a part of a family's vacation. When we did research for our book, *Teaching For Reconciliation*, we discovered that one of the strongest character-building components in youth ministry was having a meaningful service project. Some experts provided stories about how that was the most significant contributor to their adolescent development.

"Are there any strategies you suggest for blended families?"

David Olshine

I've been a part of a blended family. It can be very intense. You're bringing different baggage from different homes. You're bringing different rules. Some families are more affectionate than others. Some families are not allowed to get angry. Some are even allowed to get angry and to throw things. There are different rules on how you treat your parents in those families, so I'd say be patient. Listen a lot to each other. Communicate — up front — your unspoken, nonverbal issues that are important to you. Maybe lay it out at the beginning: "This is who we are as a family." Have different members of the family address some of their issues. I'd say communicate from the start. **Be brutally honest with each other. I think that will cause some insight, and will cause people to be much more patient with each other.**

> Be brutally honest with each other.

We did that as a family. And we started talking about how we were different. At first I don't think many of us kids liked it, because we felt like we were on the spot. But by resolving some things up front you didn't have to be forced to discover some important matters later; you didn't have to go from major crisis to crisis. We communicated from the beginning, and that resolved a lot of potentially disastrous issues later on down the pike.

Mark Senter

Parents need to develop the skill of empathizing. They need to put themselves, the best they can, inside the skin of the kids. **There is no way that they can really experience what the kid does, but I think our tendency with our kids — especially our teenagers — is to tell first, and to feel later. Empathy is what I would preach.**

Jay Kesler

This requires a straightforward, honest acknowledgement that a blended family is Plan B for their lives. We're going to make the most of Plan B. Not sweep under the rug that this relationship is the result of pain and disjuncture, even in an "ideal" sense, where both previous spouses have died, where a widow and a widower have gotten together. Even then, you've got to acknowledge that kids have feelings about their real dad versus their new dad. I think, in these families, people have got to be willing to confront, to discuss, to have family councils, and let people ventilate. Because when you don't do that, when you act like you are going to create a "Leave It to Beaver" setting, this creates an entire array of problems for the children. For instance, take two children, a boy who is 16 and a girl 14, who have no blood relationship living in the house with normal sexuality, normal attraction. Why shouldn't he be in love with her? Why shouldn't he see her as attractive? Parents and kids are going to have to discuss these topics and make provisions for them.

> About all the parents can do is hold their breath until the kids are old enough to get out of the house and start their own life.

It requires intentionality. I meet families where the kids have understood the situation really well. They don't think that you can go back and make things different. You can't change it. Let's accept it. But it takes a lot of work. **Especially when the children are older when the blend takes place, about all the parents can do is hold their breath until the kids are old enough to get out of the house and start their own life. It's not going to be a bowl of cherries.**

Dave Rahn

I think the difficulty of a blended family is that each is a different case, as it is in any family, but even more so in blended families. The relationship that all of the parents and stepparents have with their children needs to be evaluated. You have to ask them the question: "What does it take to build this new family into a good relationship?" Sometimes they're overcoming incredible stuff like bitterness and mistrust. **There's nothing about a good**

relationship that's automatic. As a parent, I'm always earning the right to influence with my child. I think it is counterproductive to ever think that I have a biological right to influence them.

RH: Well put. There's no license.

DR: Right. I can think of kids in ministry that were hard cases, and you just can't get through to them. I did everything I could do. Then something opens a little glimmer of hope in the relationship. **In local church ministry you might walk away from those tough cases and say, "That's not someone I can reach." You can't do that in a family.** It requires persevering, praying, and hanging in there. Taking a long-term perspective.

Dennis McCluen

One practical strategy is regular family meetings. **Talk about the basic issues, like rules and rituals, because they have blended different rules and rituals into this new system.** Talk about schedules, values, and decision-making. This is critical in any family, but I think in a blended family it has heightened importance.

Haman Cross

In Uganda, unlike in any other place I've seen in the world, families are taking in families. We're talking about families of seven or eight children. When an uncle dies, then a relative takes in seven, eight or nine different children. No bitterness, no complaining. It's just part of the culture and part of their thinking. Yet it is very difficult and very challenging. I would describe it as a stewardship, as opposed to ownership. We need more of that stewardship mentality.

Marlene LeFever

I think that that is one of the most difficult things that you can possibly do. I've had people tell me over and over again — who get into blended families: "If I had it to do over again, I would not." This is an issue that the church has not dealt with.

193

This is an issue that the church has not dealt with.

There is not a good enough support group. I guess I would say, make sure that you are a part of a Christian counseling group, and that everyone in the family sees that group experience as a positive, not a negative activity.

RH: Do we not have resources which are similar to the ones we use to help single parents?

ML: There's so much more going on with blended families than there is in a single parent family. But you add two families together — with different goals and it gets into this first-born, second-born, last-born syndrome. If I grew up as a first-born, there are certain characteristics that are a part of who I am, caused simply because I am first-born. You throw me out of kilter and put someone else in as first-born and instantly, at fourteen, I become the second-born in the family. What does that do to my ego? What does it do to my self image? **I'm not sure we've begun to see the ramifications of the blended family problems.**

Chapter 12
The "D" Word — Discipline

How do you approach the controversial topic of discipline? What directions can you provide to parents of teens, on this topic?

Wayne Rice

That's an easy one. **Choose your battles wisely, or you'll be battling all the time. For example, I know some parents who fight with their kids to the death over a messy bedroom.** My feeling is, hey, if that's the big issue for you, what are you going to do when your kid's doing something that is morally wrong? **There's nothing morally wrong with having a messy bedroom.** That's one of the ways kids express their identities, by decorating their rooms in "early landfill." That's their domain. That's one of the areas that they have control over. It looks like no control to us, but to them it's a statement. It's saying, "I don't have to be like you."

Choose your battles wisely.

So what I'm saying is, if you let that hair style or that music they listen to or that earring in their eyebrow — or whatever — become the main issue, then you're going to lose your kids. **Because there are going to be times when they do something** *really wrong* **and you're going to raise a stink about that, too, and you have already spent too much on things that don't matter.** So, we have chosen to pick those battles that are worth battling and let the other stuff go. And kids aren't stupid. They'll make a lot of right choices, if you just give them the freedom.

Haman Cross

You can't be a good professional athlete or rap singer without discipline. I think we need to repackage discipline in terms of lifting up people. I think discipline needs to be repackaged so it loses the negative connotation. When you talk about discipline you always see it as punishment, but the reward is there as well. We need to repackage the concept of discipline so it becomes something beautiful and attractive.

I do workshops on discipline and we talk about the four levels. The way God disciplines us — or the value of discipline in our lives — God gives us instructions. He wants us to be sure of what we are supposed to do. Then He warns us what will happen when we don't follow that instruction. When we blow it, there are things He will do or say to correct us. If we ignore the warning and reject the correction, then there is punishment. But some talk about discipline and go from instruction straight to punishment. There is a lot of energy and effort needed to warn. I mean, God will tell us to do something ten different ways. In discipline, we need to see the level of instruction, not just the level of work. That takes effort, and you have to put it at the kid's level. You have to take into account personality, temperament, and all that. But then there also has to be a warning. There has to be "here's

Don't do the crime, if you can't do the time.

what happens when you blow the instructions." To me, the kid does not really understand until they can tell you exactly what will happen: "Here are the ten things that will happen." And then, the correction. We have to walk them back through that correction.

People need to understand this whole violence trend that is going on — seeping into our country, including the church. There *are* consequences. There *is* punishment. **Don't do the crime, if you don't want to do the time.** And we've lost that. People want to do stuff and get away with it. Go back and restore. You owe the victim. And that has to be really clear, so that a very young person becomes accustomed to experiencing punishment. **We get so soft, we don't want to punish. We don't want there to be any consequences. We don't want to hurt their feelings. We don't want them to have pain. But at the same time, we don't want to reward them. We don't want to say positive things and do positive things for good behavior. We just need to repackage that whole discipline thing.**

Roger Cross

If parents haven't disciplined kids when they were younger — and taught them what discipline does and what the guidelines are — they might as well forget it when kids get to be teenagers. **I can't emphasize enough how it's so important for a young couple to be restrictive when they're young parents, when those kids are young.** Then, when kids get to be the teenagers and parents begin to give them more and more rope, it's not so bad. But that's only done if you've handled the first ten years right.

Even when kids become teenagers, the words of advice I give to a parent are: Whenever possible, predetermine the discipline. "Hey, John, you're going out tonight? Great. Got to be home tonight by, what, twelve o'clock? That's important. John, if you're not home by twelve, you know you're grounded." The discipline is determined without all the emotion. Up front. **I really encourage parents — when their kids get to be teenagers — to ask themselves, "Now, *why* am I doing this with my kids? Why am I putting this restriction on my kids? Is this really necessary? Am I really helping them to grow to be an adult?" That has to do with discipline as well.**

Len Kageler

Discipline is a teaching tool, a venue for learning, as opposed to punishment. That is an important perspective. **Parents usually**

approach their kids in one of three ways: permissive, democratic, and authoritarian. Studies show that homes in which parents maintained an authoritarian style towards their kids into middle and late adolescence were the homes where there was significant distress. Kids, as they mature, move into Piaget's formal operation stage — **"cerebral upgrade" is a term I like to use.** It's a very powerful concept. If you are still functioning in the authoritarian mode with a kid who has gone through cerebral upgrade, you are not going to have a happy kid. Because **they feel like they are capable of much more than they are given credit for.**

It doesn't necessarily have to be a one-on-one vote, but the democratic approach is so much more appropriate for kids who enter adolescence. Then, when they reach 18 or 19, the permissive approach is best, if you've done your job. It permits you to let them fly, although it's still hard. Take a look at James Dobson's book, *Parenting Isn't for Cowards*, and note the percentage of children who are strong-willed (generally the second-born). The encouraging thing in that book, however, is that his research of those 35,000 families showed that — even though a high percentage of those kids rebel in adolescence — most of them come back sometime in their twenties.

The second insight about discipline is birth order characteristics. You cannot discipline your second born (as a typical second born) the same way you disciplined your first child. You'll have a caged animal on your hands.

Helen Musick

I have a story about my father on my first date. It has to do with disciplining. **What I want to do in disciplining my kids is to teach them independence; giving them opportunities to develop their independence, choosing what's right and wrong.** When it came to the first date I ever went on, I approached my father, who was a Navy commander. He was very precise, very strong about what we do, what we don't do, when we do it, and when we don't do it, as a family. I asked him the question, "When do I need to be home?" because I had never been out like that before. To my amazement, his answer was very different from what I expected. He said to me, "You be home when you think it's time to be home." I was stunned. I was fifteen. I thought he would say "I want you home at ten o'clock, not 10:01, not 10:02, but 10:00. Do you understand me?" To which I would have responded, "Yes, sir." But instead, I was shocked, and I was home at 9 o'clock. But if my father would have said 10 o'clock, I would have chosen to be home at 10:00 because that was the boundary. **So, there was a shift in parenting from authority to parenting from respect.** I came home at a reasonable hour, because I respected my father and my mother. I respected what they thought about me, and who they were and how the family was to be run.

Rick Dunn

The number one caution is don't discipline for your own benefit. We should not discipline teenagers to release anger, to relieve guilt, or to resist discomfort. It is awfully tempting to discipline in such a way to make the parent feel better. **Improper discipline of a teenager taps into our own needs and our own issues.** But, at the end of the day, that is *not* the question. The question is: **"Does this discipline work redemptively in my child's life, to give them a better opportunity to grow into who God has made them to be?"** Redemptive means they have to take responsibility, they have to acknowledge truth. If there is sin, there is guilt. And they have to ask forgiveness. They have to make choices. They may not take that opportunity, but that is ultimately not my responsibility as a parent. My responsibility is to put that opportunity there for them, as a redemptive approach.

David Olshine

Discipline has got to be creative. "I'll ground you for life" or "you're not going to talk on the phone for the next eight months" doesn't work. We parents get really weird sometimes. My daughter, Rachel, let someone cheat off of her homework, which she

199

really didn't want to do, but did anyway. She gave in to the peer pressure. She signed my wife's name, because a lot of the time the teachers send stuff to parents to sign off on their kid's homework. Well, my wife caught this deception, and then we caught Rachel in the act of lying and cheating. Rachel's a really good student. But she felt compassion for a student who wasn't doing so well. And it nailed her. So, as parents, we went upstairs and visited with her, and she cried. **Instead of us saying, "You're not going to watch TV for a week," instead of telling her to write fifty times: "I'm not going to cheat again," we presented some scenarios to her. We gave her the power to choose some options.** She ended up calling the person who copied her stuff and apologizing for letting her cheat, and then she met with the teacher, and apologized for forging Rhonda's name.

I don't know if that's creative discipline, but it was redemptive. And it was the constructive communication that helped — making her communicate her wrong to both parties. We've never had any problems since. **I guess I'd use the word constructive discipline instead of creative.** I think that we need to use love, logic and give kids options. I've been doing that recently with Rachel, when she's done things that I'm not happy with. **I might even add a bit of humor, like, I'll say: "Here're your options: do this or do that, or put your head in the microwave."**

Dennis McCluen

The older the child gets, the more the parent needs to explain not just the *"what"* of the discipline — like you are grounded for two weeks — but they have to explain the *"why"* of the discipline — the values and beliefs that lie behind. Because **the older the child gets, the more they have to understand not only the consequence but the rationale.** Soon they will have to live by the rationale, not behave because of the consequences. And if they don't internalize the rationale, they're in trouble.

Dave Rahn

Discipline's about steering teens. Discipline for teenagers has to look different than it does when they are younger. Teens have the ability to think at different levels. They need to test their own abilities. It's much more important that I get them to understand my expectations, as well as to understand the consequences when expectations are not met. There's much more of a dialogical nature to discipline with youth. **The mistake I want to avoid about discipline is thinking that my son or daughter never has a right to understand why I'm doing what I'm doing as the parent.** Now, they may not always understand, but I always want to treat them like they have a right to know. And when that doesn't happen, I'm grieved. But I'm hoping they do understand, sometime.

> Discipline's about steering teens.

Ron Habermas: Do you actually give them that type of invitation: "I want you to know why. Ask me why"?

DR: Yes. That would be a question that I would never rebuff. I'd always try to encourage it as much as possible.

Leith Anderson

I think it's a descending scale. When your child is first born, you have enormous control over that child. You can pick a child up and move him or her wherever you choose. Then your options decrease. By the time they reach teenage years, you are functioning primarily on the basis of what you have previously done, because you have decreasing control. That is where parents need to trust their children for the investment that they have previously made in them. They can't control them the way they have previously controlled them, especially in our society.

I see parents who choose to keep complete control. They keep their children at home. I talked to a family a couple of years ago. They decided that their children — teenage children — would never be able to hear popular music, would never be present with people outside the family without a parent there. But that's just not realistic for most people. So, what they are going to have to do is allow that freedom, whether they choose to or not, then deal specifically with extreme cases, so that they have clearly set their boundaries for which there are consequences.

I think consequences are a significant issue with teenagers. What is helpful to parents is to understand that there should be consequences for behavior. That's normal; that's good; people learn that, but parents can't inflict consequences for every independent choice.

Jay Kesler

Kids need to know the rules and boundaries of their home, and parents need to keep these consistently. **Kids need to understand not only *what* the rules are, but *why* they have them.** Each child has a different temperament; you may have compliant children or rebellious children, but the main point is that the parents have to work out what they feel are reasonable arrangements, and then refuse to let a wedge be driven between them. **Most discipline problems in the home take place when the child feels he can negotiate one of the parents around the other parent. Starting to negotiate with kids who are two and three years old, creates an absolute Frankenstein when they're eighteen.** Do not negotiate with a two or three year old. Lay out the boundaries and penalties for going over them. And be consistent, just like the law of gravity.

> *Starting to negotiate with kids who are two and three years old creates an absolute Frankenstein when they're eighteen.*

Ken Davis

Discipline has to rest on the foundation demonstrated in the parents' lives, to rest on the foundation of demonstrated grace within the family. And once that's in place, discipline is very essential, particularly in the beginning years. At the time when some consider it the most cruel to discipline, that's the time when it's most essential to discipline a child: when they're young — very, very young. **I would not hesitate to slap the hand of a child who continues to head toward the electrical socket with a sharp instrument, because there's only one kind of abuse that's worse than a slap on the hand. That's an electrocuted baby.** I'm not talking about spankings that are cruel. But a whack on the butt or a slap on the hand in the right situation is often appropriate.

I watched a young little girl on an airplane smack her mother on the face at least a half a dozen times. And the mother tried to reason with her that that was not the thing to do! I wanted to go over there and handle it myself. I could have shown her that there would have been only one smack, or at the most two.

There's this whole theory that physical discipline teaches kids violence, but I think that just the reverse is true. You watch kids that grow up without guidelines — that have never been taught, and never been disciplined — I'll take the other kind of kids anyday. I grew up with spankings. I deserved them. They were not comfortable, **but the word abuse does not even come into my mind when I think about them.** I'm grateful for them today. I'm grateful for what they taught me. I'm grateful that they reminded me of the things I should and should not do.

But discipline needs to be done early. It needs to be fair. It needs to be done in love. What I mean by that is every kid always needs to understand that his or her parent's love has not stopped.

My father was outraged once because my sister had disciplined her children and then she had told them immediately "I love you, but this had to happen." He said she should never do that. He said, "If she hugs her children and if she holds them so soon after discipline, they're going to come to believe that she loves them even when they're bad." And I said, "Dad, that's the point." The love never stops. In fact, there's an interesting sidelight to that story. My dad said that one of my older sisters once wrote him and told him that she went to bed many nights believing that he didn't love her. My dad (who is the noncommunicative type of person, who didn't grow up in that kind of expressive culture) called her back weeping, and said, "I had no idea, no idea that you thought I didn't love you." So they had quite a talk about that. But that was his method of punishment: if you're bad, then I'm going to withdraw my love. **Parents must start early, be fair, and always discipline in the context of love and grace.**

Ginny Olson

Just the whole need of being consistent and being fair, and listening before you act. **I think discipline is seen as punishment, rather than discipline as participating in character formation.** See the positive slant. Listen to what is going on.

RH: Any particular strategies that you are aware of that help the parent communicate to the teen, how to be more fair, more consistent, or how to be a better listener?

GO: Negotiating the consequences. It takes a mature kid as well as mature parents. When a child realizes, "Yes, I have chosen to break our family rules," then parents and child should be able to discuss, "Okay, what are the consequences? Let's talk about that."

Harold Ivan Smith

Be cautious of disciplining a child or a teen when you are angry. **There are a lot of painful memories that I have of my dad being so angry at me, angry at the situation, that he wasn't thinking of what was best for me.** Sometimes we do need time to think about it: "Does the child clearly understand, does the teen clearly understand, why they are being disciplined?" There are a lot of nebulous rules. Sometimes what I see is that it comes to the breaking point. "We're going to let it slide this time. We're going to let it slide this time. The next time, we explode." The punishment can be way out of proportion to the behavior.

I remember one man saying the hardest thing was to punish his child, but then later to say, "I do love you, I do love you." Trying to help that child to sort out, "I don't love that behavior, but

I do love you." All it takes is a little seed to get planted within the child: "Dad doesn't really love you; he just says that." That's why I go back to that expressed love. It's such a factor in their lives. **You're turning up the volume of expressed love** when kids are around a certain group of friends that you dislike or that trouble you.

Mark Senter

Logical consequences. You let them pay the price for what they do. But you don't start this with teens; you start this when they are about two years old. If you are always rescuing them from making mistakes, their mistakes get bigger and bigger, and they are never accountable for them. **The best way to let kids make their mistakes is to let them make them when young, in less harmful context. I'm afraid that many of us parents are so controlling that we want right behavior, when what we need is right reasoning (appropriate to the developmental stage).** That is something I'm very concerned about because, frankly, kids are already making big enough mistakes that they are really going to screw themselves up. They have never had to face the logical consequences of smaller decisions when they were younger.

Thom Schultz

The best answer to healthy discipline rests in forming a relationship of love and respect. The best examples I can think of (including my own life as a young person) is that when a young person strays, the first thing that should come to the mind of that young person is not their parent's anger or retribution.

The first thing they should picture in their minds is hurt. That their action caused their parents to be hurt. If there is a relationship of love and respect that is really deep, the young person is going to bleed emotionally every time he sees his parent hurt. In fact, the very prospect of their parent bleeding should deter kids from committing the wrongful act in the first place. I can tell you that was certainly true in my own life. That was uppermost in my mind as a teenager. **When I was tempted to step out of line, the first thing that came to mind was, "If my parents find out about this, they'll be so hurt." I could see my mom crying; I could see my dad being so disappointed. That crushed me, even to think about it. It prohibited me stepping out of line to begin with.** When I did, and I saw what happened, that was the worst consequence that someone could put on me. Watching my parents walk through that pain often prevented future, unacceptable behavior.

RH: So, it's not the typical "I won't do this because of what happens when I get caught." Rather it's "what will happen to our relationship?"

TS: Exactly, and that's a long-term project. I'm telling you that's the most effective form of discipline that I know. The other tip that I give to parents and youth workers is to **play a picture game in your mind's eye of their young person who's just stepped out of line. Picture that teenager, not as a teenager, but as one of their adult peers.** They're very close to adulthood as it is, but I've found that teenagers respond well when they're treated with respect — even when they're wrong, and they've stepped out of line. **I like to look at a teenager who's stepped out of line and envision that person as somebody my own age. What would I say to them? How would I say it? What words would I use? Would I use sarcasm? No, I'm not going to do that with someone who is my peer.** I'm going to find other words to use and another tone of voice. I'm going to find other solutions to that problem than I would if I were looking at a child. I've found that strategy to work very well with adults who are approaching discipline with teenagers.

RH: So you're talking up the teen. It's self-fulfilling prophecy. In fact it gets back to another word you used earlier. It's an act of honoring kids. Mutual trust.

TS: And respect.

Dan Bautista

You can't discipline teens as you discipline kids. There has to be a difference. **I give teens options. I say, "This is your discipline A, and this is your discipline B, and this is your discipline C." I tell them what the consequences may be,** so that they know that if they break the rules they will have discipline. **Then I say, "These are your three alternatives, now which one would you want?"** It's almost like a mind game, because they always try to guess which one is the worst. And they don't want to go with the worst, and I don't give them the worst either. But I think that you have to be flexible in your discipline. Sometimes discipline A might not work well. As you spend time with them — get to know them — I think you know which one will work well.

Another component of discipline, which we take for granted from God, is the issue of grace. And I try to exercise that — to exercise God's grace over me — which I pass on to them.

Les Parrott

Discipline is always needed, and it is always to be done in the context of love. If parents find themselves disciplining in the absence of love, they need some help. **Scriptures are very clear that teenagers need proper discipline and, without it, those kids are at a major disadvantage.**

Mike Yaconelli

First of all, every family disciplines differently. Furthermore, within each family, each kid requires different kinds of responses. For example, **we live under the impression of fairness in America, and kids have figured this out — early on — that families must be fair. But things are not fair, and parents have been intimidated by this thing of "fairness." Life isn't fair.** I was normally much more strict on my first child

> Parents have been intimidated by this thing of "fairness." Life isn't fair.

207

than my other kids. That's because I didn't know any better. With my first kid, I read all the parenting books and did what they said. Now I realize that was no big deal. I didn't need to do that. So when my kids say, "You were stricter with me than you were with them," I say, "You know, you're right. Absolutely." I realize now that I was too strict, and I didn't need to be.

Secondly, I would often say, "You know, this kid is one strong-willed kid. My other kid was totally compliant. He went along with everything, did everything, was terrific. This other kid is totally rebellious." Yet what I desperately needed to not do was to compare, or to demand from one what the other one did. My first kid was your typical first kid, straight A's through high school and college. My second kid, 2.0 average all through high school; he just wasn't into it. He had dyslexia, and there were a lot of other things about him. That doesn't mean that I didn't get concerned, and that we didn't have big meetings about it. But now I look back and I see that when he was ready, he went back and made the dean's list. Got his credentials. Now he's teaching. When he was ready, he got there.

I often say to parents, "Lighten up." Discipline is very individual. That word is different than saying "relative" or that it doesn't matter. It does matter. Our kids need to know. They need to know that there are boundaries and lines. **The trouble I'm seeing with parents today is that, God forbid, parents don't want their children to be uncomfortable, or deprived, or to feel like they've been treated unfairly.** The reality is that that's when they know that they're loved; that's when they know that they matter. **When they're treated differently, that's when they know that their uniqueness is actually noticed.** That makes a difference.

Chapter 13

Recharging Your Batteries

How do you encourage parents to be strong in their seemingly endless task? How can they be reenergized?

Leith Anderson

The people that we are dealing with, in the suburban situation, are people who are highly motivated to invest heavily in their children. **Parents need permission to take care of themselves, to be told, "It's okay that you take care of your marriage. That is not neglecting your children. In fact, that's one of the best things you can do for your children."**

Ron Habermas: It's not a selfish position to take, you mean.

LA: Correct. In fact it's necessary in order to take care of your children. **When parents come to me — perhaps a couple that is distraught over the direction of their child's life — the first thing I ask them is, "What are you doing to take care of yourselves?" They are often taken back by that question, because they are not taking care of themselves, and they think that's a good thing. But it's not good.** If they end up in divorce or have a breakdown or heart attack, they're no good to their kids then. They've got to stay healthy through hard times.

> What parents often need from ... the church is permission to take care of themselves.

RH: I suspect that recharging batteries is different for different people.

LA: Yes, it's got to be customized. **What parents often need from me and from the church is permission to take care of themselves. Often, these are people who give great credence to the clergy and the church. Permission-giving and permission-withholding are significant tasks of the church.**

Mike Yaconelli

Well, it's a very simple word. **Parents also have to have boundaries. They have to have time to themselves. They have to have lives of their own. They have to be able to say "no" to their children.** Mom and Dad need to spend time together. Nowadays, it's like, "Oh my gosh, we can never leave our kids alone. We should go to all their soccer games. Go to everything that they do." The pendulum has swung the other direction. I mean we have to have lives of our own, too, do things that we love to do together, whether our kids like it or not. I think that's very important.

Also, we need not to be intimidated. **People normally don't tell the truth about their own children, anyway, so let's not be intimidated by each other.** Things like: "My kid's doing great right now. We had a little trouble with him last year, but now he's really making some headway. We just went to this conference and now he's reading his Bible." Yeah, well, he might be reading his Bible today, but who knows about tomorrow? Rather than faking it — and pretending that it's all good — we need to accept the fact that we're not certain of the future. **We are always going to be parents. We are always going to be watching our kids grow. They're never going to be out of the woods.**

Mark Cannister

I think getaways are great. I think parents need to get away; I think this is why it's so important to have some kind of extended family whether it's biological family or extended community. **For parents, I'd give them some kind of nanny system, whether that was Grandma or an uncle or just the neighbor. Give parents one night alone a week, one weekend alone a month, and one week alone a year.** One week a year so that parents can really get a chance to recharge their batteries on a regular Sabbath kind of schedule.

RH: You mentioned the word "Sabbath." Does that have significance in any theological connection — the need for a weekly time to kick back?

MC: Yeah, I think it does, and that's why I hit that weekly-monthly-yearly schedule. I'm not sure that I'd get so legalistic as to suggest that needs to be seven hours or every seven days, but I think that, **on a regular routine, we need Sabbaths. We need rests away from every aspect of our life that demands our attention, including raising our kids.** One of the real principles of the Sabbath is supposed to be reflection, typically reflection on God. We also need to reflect on how we're doing as parents, on how we're raising our kids, on how we're dealing with our finances. We need to reflect on every area of our life, including the spiritual aspect, which permeates everything. Parents can't do that very well if they never get a break from their kids, if they never get a chance to get away and reflect on how their parenting is going. I'd really emphasize that reflective aspect of the Sabbath strongly. These getaways need to be more than just a romantic cruise to the Caribbean. While you're in the Caribbean, reflect on how things are going at home and what kind of changes you might want to make when you get back.

Mark Senter

I think that the smaller affirmations, on a more regular basis, are probably more important than the big getaways. I tend to think that big getaways are fine, but they don't solve as much as we think they solve. I think it's the little getaways — more often — that maintain life.

You need to date
your spouse.
One other thing, **you need to date your spouse. Ruth and I have a time every week (Monday mornings) that we get together, and it's just our time together.** Maybe once every thirteen weeks or so I have a scheduled conflict, but I always check with her. If we're both in town at the same time, that's our time. There's no agenda. We know it's our time together. We have a lot of other times, but Monday mornings are just a special time. It's nearly a sacred time.

And one more related topic: **I think we don't understand the sabbath, the idea of shutting down and stopping the momentum of life.** That's a bigger question, but it has a tremendous impact upon your mental health and your family's health.

Dennis McCluen

Parents need to have time away — to be with other parents; to be by themselves; to build a good marriage. One of the key goals in life, if you are married, is to build a good marriage. If you don't keep working on that, your parenting skills will diminish. Be committed to growing spiritually, and that will recharge them. **You also get recharged batteries when you celebrate life.** Don't always think about the negatives. Celebrate. Lighten up.

Haman Cross

The husband and wife need some kind of training; some kind of workshop or seminar. Just like you would schedule a vacation. Something that will teach you how to recover from parenting. That has to be in the family budget. It has to be on the schedule.

We started in our church, several years ago, what we call P.O.T. fellowship (parents of teens), a gathering that gives hope, when you find out that someone is in the same boat you are. You're not the only one struggling with a teen. We interchange ideas, we cry, we pray, and we challenge. It's really essential to go through that.

And we pastors need this support too. **I have a mentor who pastors me out of Philadelphia. And I have yet, in twenty-five**

years, to call him with some challenge or problem — whether in the ministry or in parenting — that he has not gone through. That has really, really helped me. Even to know a lot of people who have gone through your same experience, and they didn't necessarily do the right thing. It can be extremely valuable. So, now you know what not to do. All parents benefit from that kind of fellowship.

Roger Cross

Some people can get recharged by sitting down and reading a book. It gives them ideas. I get recharged by sitting in a small group of people and getting the issues out. Talking through them. Others get recharged by going to a seminar and getting six practical ways to live with your teenager. Some get recharged by simply going away for two days and never seeing the kids. So my advice to parents is to discover, "What do I need personally to get recharged?" Then, find a way to get that into your schedule.

Len Kageler

Get control of schedules. Have margins in life. Every time we save a bit of time, we backfill it with something else. That just makes us frazzled; it ruins our ability to have quality time with our families, quality time with God, and quality time with ourselves. Some families are good at doing nothing. **But most Christian middle class families are going crazy right now with too much to do.**

For example, we told our kids that it was great that they participated in sports, but that they could do only one sport a year, maybe two. We're not hauling them to soccer four days a week all year. Now, some parents would have a fit over that advice because they use soccer as a way to keep their kids in athletics so their kid won't get into drugs and alcohol. In the meantime, they are running on empty as a parent, most of the time. Different families have different preferences, but I believe

You can have money, but if you don't have time, you don't have a relationship.

that **proper scheduling, creating margins in schedules, and making economic decisions that don't require working 70 hours a week are a must.** We know a couple that just got married, and they bought a Ford Explorer — top of the line — for $27,000. They both work, and work. The wife works from 7 a.m. to 7 p.m., and the guy works 3 p.m. to 1 a.m. They never see each other. They are earning enough money to pay their car payments and their nice apartment payments. But I don't give that marriage much chance. They have forfeited time. **You can have money, but if you don't have time, you don't have a relationship.**

RH: What if you have a child who has great athletic ability but perhaps not academic potential? Based on the issue of finance, down the road, do you have them work hard to develop that athletic ability in order to get a college scholarship?

LK: That's a special situation that certainly merits consideration. Maybe there could be some networking involved. Some parents feel obligated to go to every game their kid has. For them, that's what it means to be a good parent. To be there at every game. I think that, at some point, parents need a little sabbatical every couple of weeks. I know some parents who are on the verge of a nervous breakdown because they are always racing. Of course they are exhausted already, and now they are out in the freezing rain for an hour and a half, watching their kid, thinking, "Oh, I'm such a good parent." **That's a good way to get Epstein-Barr virus, or Chronic Fatigue Syndrome.**

Ginny Olson

Do something that is not attached to your identity as a parent or a spouse, but is an expression of who you are as an individual. That may be taking acting, an art class, or golfing. Something that allows you to step away and say, "I am a person, I'm not just a role." That helps with the whole "empty nest" issue, or if there is divorce or death. How do I continue my life without this person? **To set up some patterns which say, "there is more to me."**

214

Marlene LeFever

I think every parent needs to have someone in their vicinity who loves their kid and who will take them shopping or do something fun with them. Last Saturday I went Christmas shopping with a kid whose mother has cancer. We had to find the perfect gift for the mom who has cancer, and that was a very, very hard thing. But it was something special. It took her out of the home for about three hours, and we actually had fun — went to McDonalds — we had a great time. I think every child, every teenager, needs to know that there's someone they can run to when things are falling apart — who is not part of this immediate family.

Jay Kesler

It is extremely useful for churches to sponsor renewal, marriage enrichment weekends. Most couples would be helped to go to these at least once a year. Parents find out that they don't have the only strange kids in the world. In addition, many parents are worn out with the pressures of keeping up with the Joneses. Also, there needs to be room for romance and getting away. Couples with younger children can help each other by doubling up, keeping each other's kids for the alternate weekends. All three of my kids are in churches where they do that. You know, the "it takes a village" thing; churches are villages, villages of young marrieds who help each other.

> Parents find out that they don't have the only strange kids in the world.

Helen Musick

All kinds of parents have got to come together (with each other) to be recharged. There's real comfort in sharing a common ground and a common struggle. If, as a parent of a strong-willed child, for example, I find another mom that has a strong-willed

215

child, and I hear her say, "Oh, my kid said to me, 'I don't like you,' the other day too," that makes me know that I'm not alone. **If parents of teenagers were to come together and find that their struggles are not only about them, but about a natural developmental process that many parents experience, I think they would find comfort and strength.**

RH: So not only coming together as spouses to coordinate efforts, but getting together with parental peers that might have common experiences?

HM: Yes, in the church and in the community. One thing that I like to talk about in these gatherings is preadolescent counseling. Helping parents understand what are going to be typical struggles. Remind them that they went through adolescence themselves, but they've forgotten. Identify the natural developmental tasks and the ups and downs of what being an adolescent is all about. Because when I hear my teenager saying to me, as her parent: "How did you get that tattoo?" I am actually hearing something good. She's able now to make those abstract comparisons and enter a whole new level of thinking. Then, I can engage with her on a different level. I can say, "Let me tell you a story of when I was 17."

David Olshine

First, there's something to avoid: this whole TV generation — including parents — thinks that they are really getting recharged with TV — that TV really helps them relax. But I've read studies that show that TV does quite the opposite. TV doesn't settle people in, it doesn't relax them, it really stirs them up. Some people watch so much that they have trouble sleeping at night. **So I would say, learn to find some ways to relax quietly. I think that some of that involves intimacy with God. We're losing the concept of "quiet times." We're rushed. So I'd say, get back to basics, develop some intimacy with God.**

We need to rethink the value of the Sabbath.

Another idea is the concept of shabbot — the sabbath —

that's not practiced in our culture very often. Do some creative sabbath-keeping. Richard Foster says that a sabbatical in some cultures means abstaining, like taking a sabbath from food. You fast from eating for a day. Or in some college ranks, taking a sabbath (or sabbatical) doesn't mean "not working," it means exploring and pursuing new interests and new avenues of study. Recently we did a sabbatical from TV in our house, and we would just say, "On Wednesdays we're not watching TV; we're going to do something else as a family." We've kept that pretty consistently, and it's been really neat. It's not been a big loss. Also, I've started on Mondays "doing a sabbath," through recreation. I'll spend time on a Monday, more than any other day, where I will just work out. I've done another sabbath where I just decided to go out in nature for the whole day. Rhonda and I went out for the whole day. We didn't talk much, we just listened to the birds. It was a beautiful fall day. We did some hiking and ate lunch. **We need to rethink the value of the sabbath.**

Rick Dunn

Work on your marriage. Build that friendship. Take time for a date, relax, go on retreats, be creative, go to a concert or a movie. Do something you really enjoy.

The critical component is to include what I call "remembrance celebration." **God created us to be people who remember and celebrate.** Our goodness, our faithfulness, our heritage are based on these two issues. Go back to the first place you dated, when you fell in love, the first kiss. Rewatch your wedding video, renew your vows. Bring home flowers on a special day. Deepen and enrich your sense of belonging to one another.

And, if you are single, build intimate friendships outside of the home. Find people to help and strengthen you. Because we are givers to our kids, it is wonderful when we also receive support from others.

Thom Schultz

Jesus is our model. We've got to do what Jesus did. Take time out to simply seek peace, silence, and solitude. That's harder and harder in today's fast-paced society, but it remains the key — the resource — that Jesus taught us by His example. And it works.

Dan Bautista

It's good to look at what other parents are doing. Read about it. Obviously, when your batteries are not charged, it's because you're not tapped into enough energy. I think that we tend to solve our problems ourselves, but we need to share them. That happens a lot in our particular Hispanic culture because we get together as families a lot. Much more than probably any other culture. We just had our regular monthly meeting for the Hispanic Republicans of the county, and it was quite noticeable in the paper that we were really gathering in a Hispanic manner. All the way from the elderly to the little babies at that meeting. **We get everybody together; I think that's one way you get recharged. Just by being there, socializing, talking to other parents, and understanding what it means to be a good parent of a teenager.**

RH: What can you identify, of intentional design, that has helped the Hispanic community, regarding intergenerational learning and growing?

DB: We can't get away from our traditions, even though there is a lot of influence from other communities to do that. There are some trends, especially in the educational system, that don't want to have anything to do with the past. **But we need to learn from our history. There're a lot of good lessons there, like the storytelling and advice from the elderly.**

RH: So that helps because it is built into the culture?

DB: Yes, definitely. Sometimes it doesn't help, but I think it helps more than it doesn't. It helps both extremes, age-wise. Teens benefit. And the elderly need that support system, too, because it is a reassurance of their role, rather than just throwing them in a nursing home and forgetting about them.

"How do you encourage parents to be strong, reenergized?"

Wayne Rice

Well, one thing that my wife and I have done over the years on a very regular basis is to get away. Our kids know that we like to travel. And I think it's reassuring too. It keeps the romance in our marriage. **At the top of the list of good parenting, when it comes to adolescents, is to make sure that your kids know that you're totally, madly, passionately in love with your spouse. And there's nothing they can do to change that. They can't play one against the other. Anything you can do to protect your marriage, do it.** For us, it's been a matter of priorities. We get away and don't feel bad about leaving the kids with somebody. That's a good way to get your batteries recharged.

> At the top of the list of good parenting ... is to make sure that your kids know that you're totally, madly, passionately in love with your spouse.

Dave Rahn

The chance to get away mentally, physically, and spiritually. Indulge themselves in self-renewing activities, whatever that looks like. And, in that context, find some ways to help them talk, dump, and listen to both the good and the bad about their parenting. **Recharging, to me, isn't about going off and doing something totally restful and then coming back. It's about going off and doing something to get a little bit renewed.** Getting some renewed strength and renewed vigor, with a little more rest and relaxation behind me.

Actually thinking and interacting. Finding out that someone else is like me and understands my own ups and downs as a parent. And what that does is to renew you for the battle, the struggle. It's like, "Okay, I'm not alone. I've been heard. I've been understood. I've had fun. I've enjoyed somebody. And, more than that, I'm more prepared to go back into it."

RH: It's tougher for single parents, I expect. How would you do what you're suggesting, if you were a single parent? Whom would you renew with, or how?

DR: Single parents need to get another person. I think you find a kindred spirit. And that other person doesn't have to be a single parent, they just have to be someone who understands and accepts you the way you are. You can be comfortable with them. **And yet it's not about somebody who just accepts you the way you are, but who also fiercely helps you to be what you want to be. Which, to me, is the definition of encouragement.**

Ken Davis

They need to get away from their kids. Today our culture makes people feel guilty for getting away from their children. I think that they need to get away sometimes. Get a babysitter, go on a second honeymoon, take a short vacation. And I think a single parent needs to enlist some help where, a couple of times a year for two or three days, someone will take her children and allow her to recharge her batteries. This is not selfish. **Put yourself in a position to have the strength to really care for your children. There's a lot of psychology out there today that "you're first." I don't buy that. The truth of the matter is that if you're burned out, you can't help much.**

> The truth of the matter is that if you're burned out, you can't help much.

Les Parrott

I like Charlie Shedd's line that the best thing that any parent can do for their kid is be madly in love with their spouse. That's so true. Parents really do need to focus on whatever it takes for them to be recharged. Every couple is a little bit different. There're all sorts of ways to recharge. **It's easy for parents, once they have kids, to make them the center of their lives. That's a** noble thing. That's even a good thing. But their marriage needs, at some point, to take real priority over the kids. You know the old line, you can only take someone as far as you have gone yourself. If you are not a healthy parent, guess what, you're not going to have healthy kids.

Chapter 14
Waving a Magic Wand

Imagine you had the privilege to have one of your wishes granted, to benefit parents and their adolescents. What would happen to those homes as you waved a magic wand?

Marlene LeFever

I would give them the gift of thirty-five years. I would give them the gift of one day — thirty-five years from now — looking back at who their own kids have become. I'd have them move ahead thirty-five years from now, looking back at their teenager. If it's positive, celebrate. And if it's negative, then they still have time to look at that and correct it. So it wouldn't necessarily be fated. **To do what Scrooge did! Look at teenager past and teenager future.**

> *I would give them the gift of thirty-five years.*

Les Parrott

I think so many stressors in families' lives could be reduced significantly if parents just remembered the obvious: that **teenagers have a full-time job, in addition to going to school, church, and**

everything else. **Each teen's full-time job is to construct an identity. And when parents can remember that their sons and daughters are working overtime on trying to answer that question —
who am I? — parents tend to have a lot more grace for the slip-
ups and the kind of goofy things that kids can do.** Sometimes we
tend to think our teens are being lazy. **"Why are they just sitting
around in the basement playing the guitar or out in the driveway
shooting hoops?" But those are the very things that those kids
need to be doing to build that identity. Experiences that often
seem the least productive are just the opposite.** I see parents who
push their kids into being "more responsible"; they want them to
get a job and so on. Kids have the rest of their lives to work.
Sometimes getting a job is the worst thing that kids can do.
Sometimes when they get a job their grades go down, cheating
goes up, drug abuse goes up. And what a job might really be teaching is more about materialism than it is about responsibility.

Ginny Olson

**Families would have dinner together, and would have one
hour a night to connect. No TV, no phone, just have time face to
face.** I just see more and more isolation. I think it was *Time* magazine that said, theoretically, you could go to your home, drive into
your garage, push your garage door opener, and you never see
your neighbors. We're developing such an isolated culture. **We're
not connecting even with the family. How do we talk, how do we
share lives? How do we share our journey together? And those
dinner discussions don't need to be profound. It's just daily discipline. We need to communicate that we are in life together. We
count on each other.**

Dennis McCluen

There has to be an atmosphere of honesty. Denial of the
truth is the greatest problem in most families. **I grew up in an alcoholic family, and the denial there was huge. But I watch contemporary Christian families also live in denial. Like how "there is a**

pink elephant in my room," but no one sees it. You pretend like there is not one.

Ron Habermas: Give me some categories of honesty.

DM: Honesty about realistic struggles that are going on, instead of just dealing with behavior. Talk about what is going on. Parents need to be honest about their fears, their lack of training, and their love for their kids — which is assumed but not often verbalized. Kids need to hear: "We don't know what we are doing, but we're doing our best. We love you dearly, even if we make mistakes.

They need to hear: "The reason why we freaked out when you were fifteen minutes late is because we pictured you in a ditch somewhere."

The reason why we freaked out when you were fifteen minutes late is because we pictured you in a ditch somewhere."

We just don't verbalize important information. My wife modeled that for me, early on in our marriage, when I watched her sit down with our four-year-old son and apologize for her behavior. I never grew up with that. I remember thinking how that was a new thought for me. And I was mesmerized by the power of that honesty. Honesty about what we are doing, why we do it, and what we are hoping for. **Realize that we all struggle and doubt.** It is not easy to do. And there is a thin line between honesty and dumping on our kids.

Also, part of the magic wand is open communication. Christianized talk is very unhealthy. I would wish that parents would grow spiritually. Because parents are then stronger, to sustain the ups and downs of life, emotionally. **There seems to be a correlation between their own growing with Christ and the ability to withstand the pressures of being parents.**

Haman Cross

That's a tough one. I wish they knew the wisdom from the Book of Proverbs. Proverbs is a book of common wisdom, common-sense wisdom. And parents of teenagers need this practical wisdom. They need answers to: "How do I wisely parent?"; "How do I make wise decisions?" and "How do I recover in a wise way?" **I believe that practical wisdom is lost today. Too many parents don't have a clue.**

Jay Kesler

The magic wand that would cause parents to communicate honestly their feelings to their kids and give their kids a sense of adoration and love. And the seriousness of raising them to honor the Lord. **I would wave a wand over them that would say, "God has given you to us, and we're going to stick with you no matter what. You can't get out of this family. You're secure with us, and you are with God himself." I think the wand would look something like the father in Luke 15.** He would be this waiting, patient father who is willing to receive them back and put a ring on their finger and shoes on their feet and clothes on their back. **The image of the waiting father in Luke 15 is the great biblical idea of parenthood. A model of God Himself. But it also allows the realistic cause and effect to operate in the lives of the young people, even the sadness on the part of the parent. The father was not overjoyed with the fact that the kid had reached the bottom, but he was overjoyed with the lesson that he had learned at the bottom.**

Helen Musick

The picture that comes to my mind is a dinner table with the family sitting around a home-cooked meal. The TV is off, and the father and mother are engaged in conversation with the kids. Where prayer is heard. When the butter is needed, the kid says, "Sarah, would you please pass the butter?" There's a sense of respect and direction. It represents a coming together of the family. It's the only time of the day when we all share some interests. **In my house growing up, we didn't have a family altar, we had a dinner table. And that was where we learned respect for each other and respect for God. And I just don't see families do that**

today. When neighbors come in and even see me cooking a meal, and hear that we actually sit at the dinner table together, they are just amazed. **We've really tried to guard our family time at dinner. We build in traditions around our dinner table.**

Dan Bautista

Make all programs on TV more suitable for the family — to help the parents by giving them an understanding of what the secular world is trying to do. **I don't think that we need to give parents a set of seven magical steps, but perhaps we could give them seven principles of how to use TV or media. Then let them make the decisions. A lot of the problems with teenagers today have come because parents don't have a clear philosophy of life that is beneficial for the family.** One of the problems of our culture is that they have been brainwashed by the media and by the secular society. We are trying to combat that. Give them a practical understanding of what is happening around them, then let them use those tools to determine what is best for them.

Harold Ivan Smith

I would want to see churches create places where parents could be honest about their parenting skills. I see them offering programs, but sometimes it's very patronizing. What they need are places for broken parents. For parents who are really failing (or sense that they are failing), they don't need somebody who is going to jive them or beat them over the head, but someone who will say, "Yeah, parenting is a tough job today. It really is. We want to help you." I want the church to think about what they are doing when they say: "If you love Jesus, if you love the pastor, if you love the church, you're going to take part in *every one* of these activities." I think the church has to say, "Are we helping or are we hurting?"

I was in a church the other day where they finally had to say, there are now two nights every week when the church is closed. They made the decision that these are two nights people need. And it wasn't just canceling them so that people could schedule other things. It was really saying: "We want you spending time with your families." I was in one church where the pastor occasionally calls the homes of his staff members on these two nights and says, "I just wanted to see if you were home tonight. I want you home, because you are modeling, to this congregation, family values. And I need to know (and people of this church need to know) that you are home." So the church has to really ask to what degree do we take this position. **It's awfully easy to chase secular humanists and drug pushers. But to sometimes say, "Have we put too many activities and too many pressures on the family?" — that takes courage.**

Wayne Rice

If I could wave a magic wand — which I'm trying to do in our own church — I would produce mentors galore, to come alongside our kids. That's the best help I could provide parents. If I were in a church that wanted to help parents of teenagers, I'd surround their kids with all kinds of really wonderful adults. That's the magic wand that I'm trying to wave. **I'd not offer more insights into good parenting. I'd just surround them with tons of adult role models. The church is the extended family.** Parents, nowadays, don't always have the benefit of that — all these adults. **When I was growing up we had grandparents, and uncles, and aunts who all lived in the same town. And the reason I never got into any trouble is that I had too many people to disappoint. I think that was probably the best safeguard. All these people who had a vested interest in your kid became a tremendous deterrent against their negative behaviors. Furthermore it becomes a tremendous motivation for positive behaviors.** That's the magic wand. We need to provide that extended family — all these people who are crazy about your kids.

> I would produce mentors galore, to come alongside our kids.

Len Kageler

I would want to have a neon sign above every kid's head — that only parents could see. It would have the word *advice*, and it would have a neon circle around it with an "X" through it. **Kids don't need advice first. They need their feelings acknowledged first. They need to be listened to first.** Advice is okay, but only later in the process. Sharing advice first is a default mode for parents.

So, if I could wave a magic wand, and have kids display that neon sign that only parents could see, it would truly change the communication style in the home. We would see kids feeling a lot better about themselves, and a lot better about who they are as persons, a lot better about their parents. There would be a lot more self-respect, a lot more teamwork and family togetherness.

Leith Anderson

I would keep them better connected to their extended families. We have a 17% annual mobility in the United States in terms of change of permanent address. That has been one of the most destabilizing factors for families. It used to be that people would grow up and go to a religious college affiliated with the church from which they had come. They would then meet a future mate who came from that same religious background, and then they would typically, after college, return to the community where their extended family was. That provided enormous continuity in socialization. Wars disrupted this in the past, which is really difficult.

Now we're going through enormous urbanization in America, which has taken extended families from rural areas and dislocated them. That's a world-wide phenomenon. **Because the church has become the extended family for many of these people — and that's a role for which we're not always well equipped — we don't always know what to do.**

RH: So, almost one-fifth of your people are leaving annually?

LA: Well, on a national basis, it's close to that. It's actually somewhat less. I have a whole theory on this, and that is that **we have moved from *physical mobility* to *mental mobility*. We're changing our long distance carriers, and we're changing who we're married to, but we're keeping the same permanent address.** And in some ways, that's even more dangerous. **The expectations on the church are just huge. Many times, the churches just are not able to deliver what is expected of them. We do parental functions. We're parenting Baby Busters who came from dysfunctional families. They need to be parented before they need to be discipled. We need to provide job counseling for people who are unemployed. Many things that used to be done by extended families, now churches must do.**

We're parenting Baby Busters who came from dysfunctional families. They need to be parented before they need to be discipled.

RH: You say that, because of the church-shoppers mentality, the demand is higher on the church, whether it's realistic or not?

LA: The expectations are higher because they don't know where else to turn. In large part, this is very good news for the church because we are now in a position to provide direction and services that people can't get anywhere else. We have a total monopoly on these ministries to people. The schools can't provide it; the community can't provide it. Nobody else can do this but the church. So that's really great! The difficulty is that many churches are not ready to do this. They don't know how.

RH: Are there any statistics that you know of pertaining to this mobility? For example, would church "shopping" statistics make the numbers pertaining to mobility seem even higher?

LA: I'm working on a project with the Lily Endowment and, contrary to what a lot of popular sociologists say, people are not changing churches as much as is perceived. People are not changing denominations as much as it is generally perceived. They have a greater level of permission to do that but, if they can, people prefer to stay in the church they've stayed in and in the tradition from which they've come.

RH: So loyalty is both more desirable and real.

LA: Yeah. If people grow up in our church, they want to stay here, and they want the services provided. However, if they're desperate in a blended family situation, and we can't provide the services that they need, they now have permission to go elsewhere to find it. It's not because they want to; it's because they have a great need. A simple example, here, is that **parents are very concerned about the religious education of their children.** The Roman Catholic church in our area — outside of the parochial school system — often doesn't provide religious education for the children, especially past confirmation. So there are many Catholic churches here that have very inadequate instructional programs. People are now moving to evangelical churches who, if you interview them, will say to you, "I was born a Catholic, and I am still a Catholic. But I go to an evangelical church because of my kids." Some of them intend for their children, when they're grown, to return to the Catholic church. So it's with pain that they've left, but they've got to because they're going where the necessary services are provided.

RH: That's a commendable motive for parents with regard to their desire to look out for their kids.

LA: Oh, sure. I had a guy recently say to me, "Leith, I just want you to know I love God, and I love Woodale Church. But I'm still a Catholic. I don't go there anymore, but that's what I am." I need to both respect that and take advantage of the opportunity that he's provided. **There's no doubt that consumerism has given people permission to go to churches where their needs will be met. And I don't think that's all bad. In many cases, that's very good.**

Rick Dunn

I would love for parents to be working on their own growth, healing, and development. Then to share that with kids so that they are doing that, too.

I was doing a workshop on discipline for parents. At one point, I had parents talk about how they communicate with their kids. We went through twelve ways to cut off communication with your kids. Then we said, "Let's role play these ideas." So I brought a guy up, and it took him about thirty seconds to switch from what he had just said to *do* over to the things we said to *never* do. He just couldn't change old behaviors that fast. Now he could think about change and even attempt to do it, but he eventually couldn't change because of his own life patterns. And, until that dad works through those ingrained routines, he will continue to respond to his kids those ways. That's an example of challenges to growth.

Mark Senter

There are no magic wands. That's part of the mythology of this generation. There are no quick fixes — short of the Lord's return, which is the ultimate healing of everything.

RH: If there could be an ideal for you, if there could be a healing, what would it look like?

> There are no magic wands. That's part of the mythology of this generation. There are no quick fixes.

MS: The ability to confess sin. The ability to say, "I'm sorry, I was wrong." The ability to take responsibility and to repent, to turn around and go in the opposite direction. And that is a choice that can be made, and it should be a pattern of our lives, because we are sinful and we make a lot of mistakes which are not necessarily intended as sinful but have harmful effects. We need to say, "I'm sorry, I was wrong in doing that. Whether I realized what I was doing or not, I was wrong."

Dave Rahn

The number one wish would be the ability, the discipline, the wisdom, to become a great interpersonal communicator.

That's the magic wand. Let me offer myself as an example. I think that I am a pretty good interpersonal communicator when I decide to be. So, in my case, that wand actually helps to remind me that, among the things that are competing for my attention, it's not a bad strategy to put my newspaper down and focus on my kids. That's a better strategy, with shorter focus time, than an entire night of drifting in and out of the activities that I am doing and sort of listening to them half-heartedly.

RH: So, focused attention. What else does this interpersonal skill look like?

DR: The person who's listening to me — or I'm listening to — needs to enjoy talking to me. **That's how I know that I'm doing a good job of interpersonal communication: when they like talking to me.** If it seems like a chore to them, you know, like my kid saying: "I'm reporting in to Dad now," then I'm not doing a very good job. When it's fun and it's attractive, then I know I'm doing a good job.

Roger Cross

I could say something as simple as turn off the TV. I tell parents, "The most important thing in your life is not raising your kids. The most important thing in your life is your walk with Christ. The way you raise your kids, and the way you do everything else in life is going to depend on your walk with Jesus." **I think that most people — and I think surveys show this — don't take the time to grow themselves. They're not in the Word. They're just not working on their own life.** They're trying to do all the other stuff without having their own life come together. **Teen ministry is parent ministry.** Teen ministry is helping the parent grow, which will, in turn, help the teen.

I could say something as simple as turn off the TV.

Ken Davis

I would remove from parents all of the behaviors that come from what has never been healed in their own life, so that they are dealing with their children and not dealing with all the personal garbage that has never been resolved. When I spoke at Promise Keepers, I spoke on that particular topic: the hearts of men returning to their children, and the hearts of children returning to their fathers. The response was overwhelming. Tremendous pain and hurt coming out of unresolved conflicts.

David Olshine

I would remove televisions from every home for a while. See how that affects families.

In addition, I keep wondering about what it would be like to go back to the 1800's. I might even wave a wand over families to return to the 1800's, because they were much more intergenerational back then. For example, my dad lives in North Miami Beach, my aunt lives in Milwaukee, my other aunt lives in Nashville. My mom and stepdad live in Cincinnati. My sister lives in Atlanta. There's no geographical connection. So, if I could wave a wand, **I'd wave a wand to go back to the days when Mom and Dad, and Grandma and Grandpa were very closely connected geographically and relationally. I'd bring back their intergenerational focus.**

Sad to say, but when my father dies in the next ten years, my own daughter will not shed many tears, because she doesn't know him very well. I want her to be able to shed tears at her grandparents' funerals.

Thom Schultz

Both parents and teenagers would understand that the teenager is not the parents', but that each child is God's. 1 Corinthians 3:6-9 comes to mind. God looks to us to plant and water the seeds, but it's His responsibility to take those seeds and make them grow. That should change our perspective as parents. Also it's very freeing. It releases us from the guilt feelings that we feel we have to do it all, or that *we're* totally responsible for our youth. *God's* totally responsible for the harvest and for making these seeds grow. If we can see our role as parents planting a seed here, planting a seed there, watering a bit here and a bit there, then God will honor that. God will cause the growth to happen. If our kids can see it

The relationship between kids and their parents is radically different if everybody understands that we aren't owned by anybody but God.

the same way, that's freeing for them, too. **In the end, the relationship between kids and their parents is radically different if everybody understands that we aren't owned by anybody but God.**

Mike Yaconelli

We would recognize that life is hard. It takes work. And we would not, then, be discouraged when things take more time than we thought they would. The magic wand would give us all the ability to wait. I think we all try to rush things. I think parents and kids get into problems when they try to make everything happen now. We need to learn how to live in the waiting part of life.

The magic wand would give us the ability to wait.

Chapter 15
What Lies Ahead?

Identify both the hopes and the dangers that you foresee as you look at future teen and parent environments.

Ken Davis

Unless there's a change, I see chaos. Particularly in inner city homes, in places where neither parent is available, where fathers are totally out of the picture. There's a portion of Scripture that says that the sins of the father will be visited on the next generation, up to the fourth generation. **The greatest sin a father can commit is to not be there. And I believe that that sin will end in chaos unless the family structure is strengthened. Only chaos lies ahead.**

Only chaos lies ahead.

As far as the positive things, there are cycles in history. Revival comes out of need. And in modern families there is a tremendous need. But families who do pay attention are going to stick out like a sore thumb in our culture. Today, the "Leave It to Beaver" kind of family — the family that spends time together and cares for each other — is a joke. If you don't believe that, watch Saturday Night Live. **We will become the jokes of society, but we will raise people who care about each other. We will have a strong family.**

Mark Senter

You know, as I go through Deuteronomy, I read the word "remember" some sixteen or seventeen times. So powerful. Because all those memories are about what God has done. And Moses is saying, "Remember this; Remember that." So, they use these piles of rocks. They're very common, but they're designed to help us remember what God has done to rescue us. It's also to remember the people that were involved in it. **It goes back to the traditions and the celebrations. When we have stacked up memories over a period of time, this generation — probably more than any other who likes stories so well — will benefit by that strategy.**

Ron Habermas: Any dangers you see?

MS: The fear and the depression that can come from parenting. Anger. Fear can immobilize us. Fear that our kids are going to get raped or they're going to get into drugs or they're going to be dominated by Satan's music or anything like that. I think those kinds of anxieties immobilize families. **The fearful parent is an ineffective parent.**

Mark Cannister

The main danger is that we're in a relativistic, societal mode. **We're raising a generation that doesn't believe in absolute truth.** On the positive side, there's never been a relativist that wanted to be treated relativistically; so, at some point, this relativism will kind of come to an end, when people start to feel the pinch of what it means to be treated in a relative way. I don't know when that's going to happen. There's a real danger that spirituality (as well as common civility and common morality) is going to get even worse. **But I think true spirituality will come back.** I don't think it will completely van-

I think some of the hopeful signs are those signs of service and community outreach that we're seeing in this new generation.

ish or that our society will be destroyed by current trends. **I think we will rebound, and I think some of the hopeful signs are those signs of service and community outreach that we're seeing in this new generation.**

Len Kageler

The research shows that parents remain the most influential component in a teenager's life. That's the good news. Parents should not give up in despair, thinking that they no longer matter. I don't see any reason for those statistics to change. As we increasingly become high-tech as the post-industrial society that we already are, there is more and more of a need for high-touch. **The family can then become that island of civility in which its members really find comfort with each other.** I've heard some youth pastors complain that some parents are so committed to their families that the church just goes down the tubes, because the family becomes a god. I'm not arguing for that, but I think many parents err on the other side.

Haman Cross

The church, in a lot of ways, has seen that God's glory has departed. With the divorce rate, racism, and materialism, we're messed up. The Christian family is just as messed up. Two new generations are forming. One looks to the "Philistines" of the world to provide answers. **Another group I call "the Samuel generation (the faithful)" is going to restore the Ark of the Covenant.** They're going to be part of a serious spiritual awakening. I believe that Samuel was more than a priest or a prophet. He was used by God to get the Ark returned — symbolizing God's presence. We can expect part of this upcoming teen generation to do that.

RH: What gives you that hope? What signs do you see that give you that hope?

HC: As I've studied Scripture, God's tendency — when everything gets as bad as it is — God does something about it. Where sin

239

abounds, grace does much more. **It's really bad and getting worse. I just can't see God letting the game end this way. It is not consistent with His nature. God will respond to those who are seeking or moved by Him. Stuff is going to get worse, but God will get greater.** So just as the wicked kids are choosing evil, the righteous kids will choose righteousness.

Rick Dunn

One illustration of hope is all the talk about family values. What we're really saying is that **people want meaningful relationships in the home.** They may not articulate it the way we do, but there is a lot of energy being invested in that concern. There are a lot of helpful resources. There is a lot of serious interest. And there is a lot of opportunity. We live in a culture that has given us freedom to grow, and freedom to investigate these things. Freedom to live more redemptively.

Kids are made by God to want solid relationships with their parents, but they also have to deal with sinfulness and their influential culture. We can build on those facts that God is at work (in the natural realm) by the way He made kids and (in the supernatural realm) through His covenant with us. **I have natural and supernatural bases for my parenting. That is the hope I stand on. God is not going to abandon me in this process, and I'm not trying to do something against the natural way that things are supposed to work.**

What does concern me are the studies that have been done on the later effect of divorce. Kids growing up in divorced homes, after a few months, have adjusted and done well, in many cases. But as they get closer to adulthood and intimate relationships, they become less capable of productivity. They come up against issues that were not resolved for them and the brokenness that all goes with that. So they are unable to build healthy relationships and marriages. So, even if I'm doing my parenting well, my kids are going to school with kids who don't necessarily have those same resources. Parents and kids have a challenge ahead of them to hold those values tightly.

Roger Cross

I think that the Christian family is going to continue to be attacked. And it will be in terms of time. Worldly pressures are there. If we get into an era where there really is an anti-Christian emphasis, then that will put another pressure on the Christian family. **I'm not a doom and gloom person, but I do believe I see the potential for significant future conflict in our society. I don't know whether it's going to happen, but the climate is there.** It could happen.

> I'm not "gloom and doom" because I really believe "greater is He that is in you than He that is in the world."

I'm not "gloom and doom" because I really believe "greater is He that is in you than He that is in the world." So I'm sure that whenever the darkness comes, God is going to provide His light, that's going to come in different ways. **We may go underground — or whatever — but I think that God's strength is always there.** There are an incredible amount of resources out there for the Christian church. That's emerging. And if believers will take advantage of them, I think there's hope. I serve on the board of MOPS International (mothers of preschoolers) and that's certainly one of their strong beliefs. They're trying to help mothers who are in that incredibly important age. I see hope in that.

Harold Ivan Smith

There are ritually impoverished teenagers, who will eventually become ritually impoverished adults. I think the church is bending over way too far backwards to make church attractive. **I have real qualms about the seeker mentality. I don't see that anywhere in the first 1900 years of church history. I can't find seeker mentality.** What I do find, in reading the history of the church, is that faith can cost you your life; it can cost you everything. Now we're bending over backwards to make the church fun, to make it attractive, to make it cool, whatever. I even see that with funerals! I've talked to funeral directors who have people now coming for funerals, planned funerals. Families who've never been to a funeral. I've had seminary students who have never been to a funeral. They're in seminary, and they're about to graduate and lead funerals. It's that whole sense of being ritually-impoverished; we don't know how to do things, because we don't really know rituals. **It's all sort of going by the wayside, what I call the kum-ba-ya worship style of exciting worship.** And the ritual is very important.

It's what I call the kum-ba-ya worship style of exciting worship.

For instance, in my family, Christmas is this grab-and-snatch, with presents being ripped open, and nobody knows what anybody got. I was so overwhelmed when I heard a pastor talking about how, in their family, they have hats. You put the hat on and you open one present at a time. Then you talk about the gift, so it's not just ripping open presents. He said that, when they grew up, they were poor and it prolonged gift giving. But he said that that has become the ritual that is being passed on now to his second and third generation. You watch what other people get; you're interacting. It's learning rituals I think I'm really concerned about.

Another thing that I think is a good sign is that there is a hunger inside people for something as they ask: "Where am I going? What is important in my life? What is not important in my life?" Kind of a prioritizing. We're beginning to say, "Some things are not really important, but some things are *very* important." I think that is going to increasingly become an issue of people saying, "How much house do we need; how much car do we need; how much debt do we need? Do we need to do all these things?" You know, we order magazines nobody ever has time to read. I'm sitting here right now looking at a stack of magazines I have not read. Now, I'm supposed to be reading them, but I don't read them. So then I've got to put them somewhere, and I'm going to have to move them around two or three times.

I guess it's the bigger issue of how much of a consumer economy do I want to be in? We need to ask: "How can I uncomplicate my life?" Right now, there are parents out in every mall going crazy trying to buy a gift for a teenager that'll get the "Oh, wow, Mom" response.

RH: And lose in their efforts, trying.

HS: Yeah. And how do we say, "Not us. We're going to be different as a family"? It has to be through prayer. I think it also has to be through a lot of talking. If I had to say one thing, though, **if I could urge with all my being — let's get back to meals around tables.** As often as possible, meals where people talk, where people listen. Where people are not gobbling and out the door and gone. I think there's something that's starting to happen about that. It may not be fancy and it may not be great, but it's fellowship around the common listening and common sharing of food. I'm so amazed, when I read the last chapter of Paul's writings, about so-and-so showing him hospitality. Paul's work, as a missionary, was supported by many people who just simply showed the grace of hospitality.

Dave Rahn

The way change is taking place in our culture, with respect to technology, is just incredible. And I don't know what that means. Os Guiness has written, in *The Gravedigger File*, very compellingly about the implications of technology for our lives. He talked about privatization and the increase in the alienation factors between people. Technology is not going to slow down. **We have to be deliberate about the kind of people we want to be in relation to other people. That's a danger and a challenge, because the technological pace is going to continue to assault our homes. If we're not deliberate and reflective about how we use technology and how we let it affect us, it will set a pace that is contrary to healthy relationships and the reflective life.**

RH: You said technology is both a danger and a challenge. What's the challenge?

DR: Quentin Schultz says he carries a cellular phone, but it only features the phone numbers of his children. He travels a lot, but only his wife and his children know how to get ahold of him.

They're the only ones who know his number, and they can call him anytime, anywhere. I've always thought of that particular technology, and said, "I don't want a cellular phone. I don't want to be reached any more than I already am." Now he's saying that there's another way to use technology that's positive, and I'm attracted to that.

RH: So, would you respond the same way to people who say, "Trash the TV"?

DR: Yeah, **I think what really matters is what you do when you're in front of the TV.** Now, there's plenty of support to suggest that families don't do much together. I can name a couple of TV shows a week that we, as a family, sit down and watch. My kids watch and my wife and I cry. And they ask us about it — you know — "what are you crying about?" And we talk about it. It's a neat, very positive thing. **Frankly, in my memory bank, watching TV and talking about it includes some of the most positive stuff that we do in my family.**

RH: So it's not just the TV watching and the debriefing, but also the long-range issues of saying, "it's better to assess each program for the good, bad and ugly, rather than a blanket response for all TV programs." Consequently, when new programs or technology come up, you have set up a proper assessment model, as opposed to saying, "I don't know about that topic; we never had a TV in our house." It prepares for a new wave of challenges.

DR: What you're doing is you're modeling an engagement with the culture, which is very thoughtful.

RH: Didn't the Apostle Paul say something about bringing all ideas captive to Christ in 2 Corinthians 10:5? It seems to me that you can't bring "all ideas captive" by escaping them or by trashing them. You have to actually confront them in battle.

Ginny Olson

The hope is that there is still a hunger for family or community, no matter what the situation is. And my hope is that kids are

going to find that in some form. If their own family is so damaged or broken, they will look for it, ideally, in the church. Unfortunately, a lot of them are looking to gangs. But there is that kind of hunger, whatever it takes. They are admitting: "I need human contact." **I just read a student's paper on high risk behavior in teens. And the defining point was parental involvement. Kids may always be involved in high risk behavior, but it will be less dangerous if there is family involvement. It won't necessarily be drugs or sex, but it might be skateboarding, jumping off buildings, and bungie-jumping. They still need that adrenaline rush, but the restraining influence comes from the involvement of the family.**

Les Parrott

The danger goes back to my answer to your first question about this generation: apathy. Now, I have definite hope because, when I speak to parents in churches, I realize that there are a lot of good things going on. **But I think that we need to be more deliberate in cultivating hope, because hope is the answer to apathy. And the reason the kids feel like zeros, the reason that kids are apathetic, is they have no hope.** The Apostle Paul called it hope, the anchor of the soul. If you are ever going to help somebody who is apathetic, it's going to be by giving them an anchor of hope, something that will ground them. Allow them to have vision. That doesn't happen through necessarily making more money, or providing more things for them, or moving into a different neighborhood, or whatever it is that we think would help our kids more. That happens by the attitudes that we cultivate.

RH: Given that there is some objectivity to teen's worries, how do you present hope? How is the hope built when there are some legitimate concerns for apathy?

LP: Well, you need to recognize that, even though this generation feels that way — it's understandable and we need to validate that — every generation has had their own fear of how terrible things were, even in the idealistic picture we have of the 1950's. We had the atomic age, the nuclear age. The threat of the Iron Curtain.

Look at Vietnam. Addressing these things is what builds character. Seeing hope, in spite of some pretty dismal circumstances, is what allows us to rise above those challenges. **We must build courage and character in the lives of our young people.**

Marlene LeFever

The danger is, of course, the world spinning out of control in so many different ways. What will the future hold for them in terms of security — global security and global disaster? What about the national debt? **I've heard it said that the national debt is so big now that if every sesame seed on every Big Mac ever sold was worth one dollar, it wouldn't come close to paying it off. That's pretty incredible!**

> The national debt is so big now that if every sesame seed on every Big Mac ever sold was worth one dollar, it wouldn't come close to paying it off.

RH: Who has time to count sesame seeds?

ML: I don't have any idea. So, I would say that that's going to be a problem. They're not going to have any money. **Their parents, Gen Xers, are now paying a higher social security tax than any other generation. They're paying twenty times more than their grandparents did fifty years ago. What are these kids going to do? They'll have no social security.** And the economy is less than it has been. They have less potential than my generation. That can be a challenge. Marriage is no longer considered to be the only option. What do I do with alternative lifestyles? That's a challenge. **The largest private employer in the U.S. used to be General Motors, but now it's Manpower. Everything is temporary, even the kind of work that I can get. The church is even in such transition that — even in my own church — I can't count on security. I don't know that the church will be there for me in twenty years the way it was with my parents.** I can't go back to roots because I've grown up without them.

"Identify both the hopes and the dangers that you foresee."

I think that Christianity tends to go in cycles, with some of us being very inner-directed, then the world changes in some way and then we become very outer-directed. I think that these kids will grow up in a more outer-directed pattern. We've gone about as far inward — "Me, me, me, me" — as we can get. Something has got to happen to bring us back to a more corporate feel of who we are. Maybe even to the rise of denominations again.

RH: How about hope?

ML: The horizons are unlimited. That's kind of fun. What kids can do with a computer, what they can do internally with content and ideas. But again — the flip side of that — they can turn reality into anything they want reality to be. So depending on how you see that and how you use that, it can either be a hope or a devastating negative.

RH: Anything else you want to say that we've missed?

ML: It'll be fun to see what kind of music they come up with. We've run a lot of gamuts, and grunge is on the way out. What do we do now? What will this generation do for music? And if they're highly creative, we may have a whole new music and art form just over the horizon as they head into their twenties and thirties. That'll be fun to see.

Jay Kesler

I see tremendous amplified problems with the Internet, with pornography for example. There's a certain degenerate quality to some of this technology. I don't think that the human mind can recover from certain exposures. We're going to have an increasing number of young adolescent boys exposed to levels of pornography, all for the protection of "freedom" on the Internet. We're going to see aberrations that we've never dreamed of before. It's going to start hitting the press and the courts. Behaviors that are stimulated by this technology. **There is nothing in *Playboy* or *Hustler* that begins to come to the edges of the stuff that kids are going to be exposed to on the Internet. That's the greatest fear in my mind.** On the other hand, a positive in my mind is the self-conscious intentional reaction of the church to the breakdown of family and society. A very commendable response on the part of the church. I get to so many churches where they are really working on these issues, and the young couples who understand the modern world. They are not aliens; they are products of the modern world. They have decided to do something about it, and this encourages me beyond words. Nothing like this happened in my generation. We lived by that old song, "Doing what comes naturally." We just thought everything would turn out okay; these kids know it won't turn out okay if they aren't careful. I'm very impressed with what is happening. **I'm not negative about what is happening in the church as far as families are concerned.**

Mike Yaconelli

We actually believe things are going to get better. But they're not. They're going to get much worse. The reason I say that is not because I'm pessimistic. That may sound negative, but I'm hoping people will say, "Okay, things are not going to get better." **We're not going to sprinkle something over the culture and elect a Christian president. Cities are going to get meaner and meaner. It's going to become more and more dangerous to live in this country. Therefore, we have to take responsibility for our own lives and realize that this is a hard, dangerous, scary world that we live in.** Take responsibility for our part in it. **For example, what would make a radical difference in my kids' lives that would take almost nothing to do? Get rid of the TV. That would be a huge step in the right direction. I'm not saying that it is evil. I'm saying that it has so many influences on our kids that we can't even count them. It's a whole different world. It's recognizing that I am the one who has to make a difference in the lives of my kids, not some program.**

> We actually believe things are going to get better. But they're not. They're going to get much worse.

"Identify both the hopes and the dangers that you foresee."

RH: Any sign of hope?

MY: More and more people are recognizing, and finally saying, "Wait a minute, I do matter. I can, in fact, make a difference in the life of my child. I do have the skills already. I can actually make some decisions that will, in fact, radically affect my child. I can do that." I think people are disillusioned enough with government programs, seminars, crowds, systems, and psychologists. They're now beginning to go, "I can do this."

RH: It's a revival of sorts.

MY: Yeah, but certainly not in the traditional sense.

Helen Musick

There has to be a shift in our understanding of freedom. Freedom today means no responsibility, no accountability. Unbalanced independence. But from what I understand of Scripture, freedom is truth. **We have to know what the truth is with regard to family and culture, understand the plumbline of truth from God's Word — what God's vision is for family, for parents, for marriages, and for being a follower of Christ.**

David Olshine

I think you're seeing right now some of what is going to happen in the future. A posture of introversion toward the media, for instance. I'm scared because I don't know that the church has got a grip on it. Also, **I think the church is in left field about what to do with Generation X kids.** There are a few churches that know what to do, but I think that our methods are old. **I think that a lot of us Baby Boomers are out of touch.** I think we can teach Bible, teach good old stories that we used back in the old days. But I think that there needs to be a whole new wineskin for a new time. Leith Anderson talks about thinking futuristically about things that we don't even know how to think about. Which is really problematic. You know, angular thinking. For example, a church recently talked to me about coming on part-time staff. The pastor and the associate

249

pastor met with me, and they were just really upset because they couldn't convince the church budget committee that they needed more help. But the staff was convinced of the need. I said, "Well, why don't you just go to two or three individuals and see if you can't raise the necessary funds?" They looked at me like, "Gosh, why didn't we think of that?" I think we need to be innovative for the future. I'm concerned with the glut of books on parenting that don't seem to be helping. **Families are really screaming for help.**

Families are really screaming for help.

RH: What do the new wineskins look like?

DO: One of the new wineskins might come with the diminishing of youth groups. We've created a youth ghetto. That's what youth groups are today. I think that some of these youth groups are problematic because they are so much into themselves. They don't really want to make a difference; they don't want to do anything. They just want to be entertained. **I think that we need to put these groups to death.** Move more to a family-based, intergenerational ministry where all ages of people are really getting in touch with each others' issues and going out and doing ministry. **I think we need to shut down some church programs and provide more free time.** I'm thrilled to see some churches stop saying, "We're busy every night of the week." We also tend to say, "Let unchurched people come to us, we'll devise the program for them."

What scares me is that **I can honestly say that I don't know my neighbors. I say hello to them, but I don't know their last name. They don't know my last name. We don't know each other. Our culture is increasingly growing introverted — Bat Cave mentality. Everybody drives up to their house at night, they push the garage door button, they drive in, and it shuts down. They're locked in for the rest of the night.** We become less prone to really meeting other people's needs. And that frightens me, it really does,

Our culture is increasingly growing introverted — Bat Cave mentality.

because I don't see the church getting more innovative, I see the church becoming more isolated. **We're waiting for the rapture to come. We're going to get out of this mess. I think that a lot of churches are dying. I think the church needs to really think through family life. What does that really look like in the 21st century?**

Dan Bautista

Again, the bad trend I see includes **things like the media, the culture, and the educational system, which have undermined our values and our traditions. I think that that's probably what will hurt teenagers most in the future.**

RH: Give an example of the educational system undermining values.

DB: In our schools they teach our kids all kinds of controversies in sex education. They don't stay within abstinence. Actually, for a lot of us, it would be better if they didn't teach any sex education until, perhaps, the last year of high school. But because of the media, and everything else that is going on, they have to teach these topics earlier and earlier in life. But leaders in Austin, Texas — away from our Valley — might not share our values, so people from our Catholic and Protestant cultures should demand more teaching on abstinence.

The other negative issue in the homes is economics. I think our teens need to learn more about the implications of not only getting a good education, getting a good job, but what it means as far as the economic impact on their own pockets — in the region, in their communities, and in their churches. They need to understand that their taxes they give to the government and the money they give to the church affects them one way or the other eventually. They need to be more informed about that. **Our hope is that they will become more fully aware of their surroundings in terms of politics and in terms of society, so that they can make better decisions and elect, then, the best leadership — whether it be at the local church level or in the schools or in the local government.** I think that they are seeing that more and more. They are

251

questioning some of the issues. They are questioning some of the roles of the federal government and of local government. They don't just sit there and take it. They are becoming more involved. Our challenge would be to inform them well and give them a good framework by which they can make decisions through that grid for life. **So that's our challenge, because we will not be able to be there to make decisions for them all of the time.** That's just not possible, and not logical either. But, **we can give them a good grid by which they can evaluate what's happening around them and give them sound principles by which they can make decisions for their life.**

And that's also our role as parents. We parents need to give teens a good understanding of economics and its spiritual aspects. The church needs to instruct in the moral and social issues. How we can affect society and become more involved in that process?

Leith Anderson

Well, on the positive side, **I think God created us to be in families. I think families have been around for a very long time, and I don't think that any of the diseases of society that we bemoan are really capable of doing away with families. Marriage is going to continue.** I hear people say, "Well, we have a gay-lesbian agenda. We have a ruling in the Hawaiian Supreme Court about gay marriages." Well, it's going to take a lot more than that to do away with marriage and heterosexuality in families. These things are not going to substantially change the family.

Now, at the same time, there are huge problems that are being faced today. **The rapidity of change is probably unprecedented. A shortening of generational span. It used to be that one generation was not a whole lot different from another generation. Today, the music changes, the technology changes; generations are really getting short. As you were indicating earlier, you may be raising an older child in a different generation than you are raising a younger child. That's formidable.**

"Identify both the hopes and the dangers that you foresee."

Wayne Rice

Well, I wish I could paint a rosy picture. I don't really see one. I think that the postmodern family is in trouble. Have you read David Elkind's new book, called *Ties That Stress?* The subtitle is *The New Family in Balance.* It focuses on what's happened to the family, how the family has changed, and how parents today are so much more selfish than before. Whereas the old nuclear families were weighted in favor of children, the postmodern families are heavily weighted in favor of the parents, the adults. We look after our own needs first, and our kids second. That's the root of a lot of problems that Elkind sees. He tries to paint a positive, hopeful picture, at the end, of where we need to go. To create a new model for the family.

But I think families, despite the hopeful word of some, are going to continue to come up short of what a family ought to be from a biblical standpoint. That poses some tremendous challenges for all of us who are involved in the church. How do we work with this trend? We're not going to turn the clock back. We're going to have to find new ways of providing a healthy environment, in spite of the fact that the world is going to become a less hospitable place and a more dangerous society in which to raise children.

My point is, unless we're proactive, unless we break the cycle, it ain't going to happen. Unless there's a way of stepping in there and saying, "It stops with me," that downward spiral is continuing. **I would encourage parents, youth workers, and family workers — anyone who cares about the family — to take action. We can't wait around for somebody else to do it.**

Thom Schultz

The world is becoming quite complex, and I think more so than we first might realize, since we're in the middle of it. There are so many options and choices available to all of us today, both adults and young people. **We need to develop a generation of parents and young people with a long-term view.** We need to sit down and really think through our goal as parents. What is your goal for your child? As young people, what's your goal? That thought process begins to put a lot of the chaos and the options we face into perspective. It begins to rank them in terms of priorities. If we can keep that goal firmly in mind, we can slice through some of the distractions. We can avoid the tyranny of the urgent. We can really begin to simplify and focus on our goal.

Everything that's being said about the influence of peers, school, media, society, technology — everything that is a part of life today — **it is still true that nothing comes close, in terms of influence, in a teenager's life to the parent. It's admitted by the kids themselves, in lots of studies. Parents are *that* important.**

RH: Take it a step beyond. You've mentioned this concept of long-term view many times. TV programs set up a major social problem and then resolve it in twenty minutes. It's instantaneous; a microwave society. How do you help the parents or the teens to say, "Hey, let's do the opposite"? How do you actually get to them and say, "You're being lied to here. This is not the road to take"?

TS: It's a whole new mindset. It's not an easy thing to turn that influence around, I know. The ultimate short-term view, for the world, is teenage suicide. I think we've got to struggle — all of us — to refocus. Let me give you an example of how this comes into play with young people. Take education. All of us, young people, parents and educators themselves, are easily distracted into looking at the short-term goal in education — whether it's the grade for that paper, or that assignment, or choosing what specific course to take, or whatever. It's fascinating to stop and ask, "What are we doing this for? What's the goal of education?" Watch people squirm and struggle with that and see how little they've thought about that question. What's the goal? Is it to get the grade? Is it to get that piece of paper? Is it to get into a certain college? Then what? Is that the goal? What's the goal? **Until we begin to step back, as God's people, and really begin to ask the big questions, we can't very well discern how to answer the little questions that come up every day in life.**

Conclusion

"My mother had a great deal of trouble with me," Mark Twain once confessed — then quickly added, "but I think she enjoyed it."

Sounds like the testimony of many naive teens, doesn't it? Or, perhaps, really bright youth!

On another occasion (this time looking at adolescence from the *other* end of life) Twain reportedly advised: "When a child turns twelve you should put him in a barrel, nail the lid down and feed him through a knothole. When he turns sixteen, plug the hole." Among other matters, I'm curious to know exactly what types of run-ins Twain had with teenagers of his day which caused such contentious comments.

Although we each will have our fair share of such run-ins with youth, I'm pleased to know that parenting — of any age child — is not a hopeless endeavor. More specifically I believe that, in the final analysis, several of this book's interviewees put their fingers squarely on the life-giving pulse of Christian leadership in the home.

For instance, recall these four quotable quotes:

Mark Senter recommended: "The '**calling to parenthood**,' for Christian families, is something that should be explored."
Mark then suggested one reassuring idea he wished was part

of that "calling": "The fact is that **my success [as a parent] is not judged by how my kids turn out.**"

Leith Anderson likewise echoed: "God is the ongoing and ultimate parent. There's great comfort — when your children don't turn out as you chose for them — to recognize that **God had other children in Scripture that didn't turn out as He chose for them**, as well."

Haman Cross extended those first two comments by emphasizing: "**Help your teens to hear God's calling**. . . . I've been used by God and I'm going to run my race. But one thing I've got to do before I leave is that **I've got to anoint the next generation.**"

Finally, Roger Cross offered one practical solution, by counseling: "Create an environment in your home where questions are acceptable. . . . **if I can't ask questions, then God isn't who He says He is. We don't have to be afraid of any questions.**"

But in these highly stressful days of Paducah, Jonesboro, and Springfield, "Can't we do something more?" an anxious parent might ask.

"Yes, I think there is more we can do," I would counter. And **it starts by reading the Bible again for the first time**. Read it anew. Read it with a teachable, prayerful spirit. Read it with the cultural needs of twenty-first century parenting in mind. Read it to customize — not compromise — God's *Word* to the *world* you live in.

How?

Permit me to share one useful analogy as an example. It is a concept based upon an actual, historical reality from the Old Testament.

But before I proceed, I must hasten to state some cautions up front. Christians need to inductively discover the basic *principles* of Scripture (from these types of historical realities), while also realizing their limited, *illustrative* nature. Conversely, they must avoid attempts to transfer any and all qualities of the past into the present by utilizing overly-literal forms of interpretation. Therefore, I want to reemphasize that what I am proposing below is *one figurative way* of viewing *one biblical concept*, while still valuing the historicity of Scripture.

Having noted these restrictive guidelines, I now want to introduce a liberating thought — something I believe is **the very best biblical picture of what the Christian family could (and should) be like in the next century: The Judeo model of "Cities of Refuge."** Furthermore, it's the same image that could be utilized by evangelical churches, Christian colleges, camps and conference centers, mission agencies, and the like.

Back in Joshua's day, God commanded that six literal cities in the Promised Land were to be designated as "Cities of Refuge." Their primary purpose was to serve as a sanctuary, a haven of refuge, for the person who accidentally killed someone. This runaway — fleeing those who would naturally want to avenge the victim — was to receive a fair trial and subsequent protection in any one of these half-dozen locations. Notice God's command for these Cities from Joshua 20:1-9 (NIV):

> Then the LORD said to Joshua: "Tell the Israelites to designate the cities of refuge, as I instructed you through Moses, so that anyone who kills a person accidentally and unintentionally may flee there and find protection from the avenger of blood.
>
> When he flees to one of these cities, he is to stand in the entrance of the city gate and state his case before the elders of that city. Then they are to admit him into their city and give him a place to live with them. If the avenger of blood pursues him, they must not surrender the one accused, because he killed his neighbor unintentionally and without malice aforethought. He is to stay in that city until he has stood trial before the assembly and until the death of the high priest who is serving at that time. Then he may go back to his own home in the town from which he fled."
>
> So they set apart Kedesh in Galilee in the hill country of Naphtali, Shechem in the hill country of Ephraim, and Kiriath Arba (that is, Hebron) in the hill country of Judah. On the east side of the Jordan of Jericho they designated Bezer in the desert on the Plateau in the tribe of Reuben, Ramoth in Gilead in the tribe of Gad, and Golan in Bashan in the tribe of Manasseh. Any of the Israelites or any alien living among them who killed someone accidentally could flee to these

designated cities and not be killed by the avenger of blood prior to standing trial before the assembly.

Children and teens, today, figuratively take the role of the refugee. They face incredible stressors and an unprecedented pressure from the outside world — comparable to the innocent victim of old who was relentlessly pursued by an avenger. Contemporary "avengers" include the evils of drugs, violence, sexual temptations and disease, to name just a few. What a powerful image the ancient City of Refuge provides today. **A commendable goal of every twenty-first century Christian home, then, encourages parents to provide symbolic Cities of Refuge for their kids.** Employing this strategy as a metaphor yields a half-dozen functional principles, based upon Scripture.

First, Cities of Refuge in the Christian family must be **visible**. Historically, at least five (if not all) of these six cities were located in the hill country or on plateaus. That is, these locations were selected, in part, because they were seen from a distance. Symbolically interpreted, this means that the contemporary home must be quite public and evident to all. It must be ready to serve those who dwell there. They must be visible and able to do what good homes do — nurture their members. They must be recognized in their neighborhood as those who stand for God and good. This "City on a Hill" analogy was also selected by Jesus, then connected with "the light of the world" illustration in Matthew 5:14. By way of application, each parent must ask him/herself "What witness does our family have? How are we described by both insiders and outsiders? How visible are we?"

Second, as Cities of Refuge, families of faith should be **approachable**. Deuteronomy 19:2,3 states that the Israelites were to "build roads to [these cities]." This was a highly unusual command for that less civilized day, especially given the Cities' location in the high country. Parents of contemporary homes must also build symbolic roads of accessibility. We must construct pathways to our kids. This means that (in comparison to the first principle, which partially focuses on being "able" to serve), parents should be *willing* to minister to their teenagers' needs. "Roads" of availability include pathways like good listening and friendly communication, in which moms and dads often take the initiative. Furthermore, these "roads" must be consistently maintained and repaired, analogous to the fact that no meaningful relationship is ever taken for granted. What "road construction" and "road repair" have you recently completed, in your family relationships? Would your kids say that you are approachable or not?

Third, nurturing Christian homes will be known as **hospitable**. Someone once defined the home as "a place to go to fail safely." Hospitality means that we must turn our homes into hospitals — to mend the hurting or heal the sick. Of course this call for hospitality reaches beyond the confines of its own membership. Not only teens who live in the home, but also their friends, should receive such humane, dignified treatment. As parents, we must constantly remember to put out the welcome mat. Joshua 20:9 recognizes that these Cities were to serve "Israelites or any alien [i.e., a non-Israelite]." There was to be no prejudice, no bias. Joshua 20:4 adds that the elders of these select sites were to meet such runaways at "the entrance of the city gate" and then to "give [them] a place to live with them." That's hospitality. And it doesn't take much effort for your children's friends to say, "Wow! Your home is really different!" In fact, every time we hear such comments at our house — based on Mary's home-cooked meals or snacks, a clean house, an inviting conversation, or other evidence of hospitality — we are regularly surprised (and humbled) by these remarks. For, oftentimes, it's the little things that count. Ask yourself if your kids and their buddies feel comfortable to "kick their shoes off and stay awhile" — always a good test of hospitality.

Fourth, Cities of Refuge were to be **invulnerable**. They were required to protect those who came to them. How relevant! Numbers 35:9ff admonishes City leaders to support those who committed these life-taking crimes unintentionally. Then, verse 25 broadens this command, stating, "The assembly must protect the one accused." For twenty-first century homes, the word "assembly" is particularly significant. Because not only parents are called to protect; *all* family members should guard those under our roof. Consequently we must be prepared to answer the question: "How are we all protecting those 'within your gates'?" Part of that protection means that we must be a haven of physical protection. Also, our kids need to feel secure emotionally, psychologically and spiritually. That is, they must sense an environment of trust. Can they freely raise any issue they want — even doubts about their faith — without being criticized? Would your children be quick to characterize your home as a safe place? Be careful of false conclusions that claim that just because you do protect your kids physically that subtle categories — like parental sarcasm of your child's behavior — don't matter.

Fifth, contemporary Christian residences need to be **reasonable**. Impartial. Unfairness is a double-edged sword: oftentimes, we parents either jump to conclusions, on one hand, or we overlook wrongdoings, on the other hand. Against that backdrop, prudent domestic leaders will counter these imbalances by providing the benefit of the doubt (i.e., not judging teens prematurely) and by exhibiting "tough love," respectively. Cities of Refuge were to offer fair trails to all runaways. They were never to be characterized by presumption, speculation or injustice. Could your child accurately claim that *any* "trial" they've had at home was unfair?

Sixth and finally, when it comes to serving its teens, parents must be **responsible**. In particular, they must be selfless, seeking the very best for their loved one. Joshua 20:6 records that the final purpose of these Cities was to eventually have the refugee "go back to his own home in the town from which he fled." Symbolically, this means "letting go" of our teens, and this gradual process must begin when the teenager is very young. It begins by including kids in various life-appropriate decisions, by teaching them individual responsibility and by instilling in them the ultimate goal of social interdependence — a healthy give-and-take between every mature believer. Negatively put, it's about avoiding codependency of any kind. How would you grade your efforts here? How would a stranger assess the maturity of your child when it comes to these matters of personal growth and accountability?

In sum, realize what Cities of Refuge are *not*, as well as what they *are*. They should never become some nostalgic flashback to "the good ol' days." Nor should they resemble a "hothouse" structure, indicating an isolationist mentality. To the contrary, these Cities — like nothing else — must advance the grace of God. Never hidden from view, these sites of mercy must also display both private and public expressions of uncommon goodness, fairness, and self-sacrifice.

I am thoroughly convinced that, if even a small percentage of committed contemporary Christian families breathed new life into this ancient yet potent "Cities" design, nonbelievers would undoubtedly repeat the very same testimony that was attributed to the early church in Acts 17:6b, at Thessalonica: *"These who have turned the world upside down have come here too"* (NKJV).

May the Lord enable us to reconstruct these bold, innovative, and biblical patterns for parenting as we quickly enter the next millennium.

Bibliography
References Cited

Covey, Steven. *Seven Habits of Highly Effective People.* New York: Simon and Schuster, 1989.

Davis, Ken. *How to Live with Your Parents without Losing Your Mind.* Grand Rapids: Zondervan, 1988.

Dobson, James. *Parenting Isn't for Cowards.* Dallas: Word, 1997.

Dodd, Elizabeth. *Marriage to a Difficult Man.* Philadelphia: Westminster Press, 1971.

Elkind, David. *Ties That Stress.* Cambridge, MA: Harvard University Press, 1995.

Fulghum, Robert. *All I Really Needed to Know I Learned in Kindergarten.* New York: Ivy Books, 1989.

Glenn, Steve H. *Raising Self-Reliant Children in a Self-Indulgent World.* Rocklin, CA: Prima Publications & Communications, 1988.

Guiness, Os. *The Gravedigger File.* Downers Grove, IL: InterVarsity Press, 1983.

Habermas, Ronald. "Cities of Refuge: An Old Testament Model for Safe Youth Groups." *Youthworker* (Spring, 1995): 88-92.

Habermas, Ronald, and Klaus Issler. *Teaching for Reconciliation.* Grand Rapids: Baker, 1992.

Bibliography

Huggins, Kevin. *Parenting Adolescents*. Colorado Springs: NavPress, 1989.

Kageler, Len. *Teen Shaping*. Old Tappan, NJ: Revell, 1990.

Lobel, Arnold. *Fables*. New York: Harper & Row, 1980.

McDowell, Josh and Bob Hostetler. *Right from Wrong*. Dallas: Word, 1995.

McPherson, Miles and Wayne Rice. *One Kid at a Time*. El Cajon, CA: Youth Specialties, 1995.

Munsch, Robert. *Love You Forever*. Scarborough, Ontario, Canada: Firefly Books, 1986.

Parrott, Les. *Helping the Struggling Adolescent*. Grand Rapids: Zondervan, 1993.

_____. *Love's Unseen Enemy*. New York: Harper, 1996.

_____. *Once upon a Family*. Kansas City, MO: Beacon Hill Press, 1996.

Phillips, J.B. *Your God Is Too Small*. New York: Macmillan, 1967.

Rushkoff, Doug. *GenX Reader*. New York: Ballantine Books, 1994.

_____. *Media Virus*. New York: Ballantine Books, 1994.

_____. *Playing the Future*. New York: HarperCollins, 1996.

Schlessinger, Laura. *How Could You Do That? The Abdication of Character, Courage, and Conscience*. New York: Harper-Collins, 1997.

_____. *Ten Stupid Things Women Do to Mess Up Their Lives*. London: Headline, 1995.

Veerman, David. *Parenting Passages*. Wheaton, IL: Tyndale House Publishers, 1994.

About the Interviewer

Ronald T. Habermas

Ron Habermas has served as McGee Professor of Biblical Studies at John Brown University in Siloam Springs, Arkansas, since 1993. Prior to that he was on the faculties of Columbia Biblical Seminary in Columbia, South Carolina (1988-1993) , Liberty Baptist Theological Seminary in Lynchburg, Virginia (1983-1988), and Okanagan Bible Institute in Kelowna, British Columbia.

He has also held pastoral appointments at the First Baptist Church in Stockbridge, Michigan, and Trinity Baptist church in Kelowna, British Columbia, where he served as Director of Christian Education.

Ron earned his B.R.E. in Christian Education, Greek and Bible from William Tyndale College, his M.Div. in Pastoral Ministries and Christian Education from North American Baptist Seminary, his M.A. in Church Ministries from Wheaton Graduate School, and his Ph.D. in Education Administration and Curriculum from Michigan State University.

Ron has authored or coauthored five books prior to this including *Jesus Didn't Use Worksheets: A 2000-Year-Old Model for Good Teaching; Down but Not Out Parenting: 50 Ways to Win with Your Teen; Tag-Team Youth Ministry: 50 Practical Ways to Involve Parents and Other Caring Adults; How We Learn: A Teacher's Guide* to *Educational Psychology;* and *Teaching for Reconciliation: Foundations and Practice of Christian Educational Ministries.*

He has contributed chapters to several other books in the fields of education and youth ministry. Additionally, he has written articles for such publications as *Christian Century, Christianity Today, Religious Education,* Youth Specialties' *Update* and *Youthworker, Group* and *Christian Education Today.*

Ron is married to Mary and has three daughters, the youngest in middle school.